Living Faiths

Sikhism Teacher Guide

Julie Haigh
Series Editor: Janet Dyson
Consultant: Robert Bowie

OXFORD UNIVERSITY PRESS

Contents

Scheme of Work

This table shows links to themes in RE across the six faiths in the *Living Faiths* series, so that you can easily navigate through the series and teach by religion or by theme. The themes are organized alphabetically under the two headings, **Beliefs** and **Moral and Ethical Issues**.

	Buddhism	Christianity	Hinduism	Islam	Judaism	Sikhism
Beliefs						
Faith origins	Overview, 1.1	Overview	Overview, 2.1	Overview	Overview	Overview
Festivals / Celebrations	2.5, 2.6	3.5, 5.2	3.2, 3.3		2.6, 3.4, 3.5, 3.7	2.6, 3.4, 3.5
Food	5.4		4.4, 4.5	3.3, 3.5	3.2	3.6, 3.7
God / Divine		1.1, 1.2, 1.3, 1.4	1.1, 1.2, 4.6	1.2	1.1, 1.3	1.1, 1.2
Key teachings	1.3, 1.4, 2.3, 2.4, 3.4	1.3, 1.6, 2.2, 4.4, 4.7	1.3, 1.4, 1.6, 3.1, 3.4, 3.5, 4.1	1.1, 1.3, 1.5, 3.1, 3.2, 3.3, 3.4	1.2, 1.4, 1.5, 2.2, 2.5	1.3, 1.4
Life after death	1.6, 2.6	2.5, 2.6	1.3	4.1, 4.2	4.2, 4.3	1.4
Places of worship	2.7	2.5, 3.2	2.5	2.5, 3.4	3.3	3.3
Religious leaders	4.3, 5.5, 5.6	2.3	1.5, 2.4, 2.5, 3.1, 4.2	2.2, 2.3	1.5, 2.7	2.1, 2.2, 2.3, 2.4
Religious symbols / Dress	1.5, 3.3	3.1	2.1	3.6	3.6	3.1, 3.2
Sacred texts	2.1, 2.2	2.1, 2.2	2.2, 2.3	2.1, 2.4	2.1, 2.2, 2.3, 2.4	2.5
Worship	3.1, 3.2, 3.3, 3.5	1.5, 2.4, 3.2, 3.3, 3.4	3.2, 3.4, 3.6	1.3, 1.5, 3.1, 3.2, 3.3, 3.4	3.1, 3.3	3.3
Moral and Ethical Issues						
Environment / Animal rights	5.4	5.4	4.4, 4.6, 4.7	4.5	4.6	4.2
Evil and suffering	1.3, 1.4	4.3, 4.5	4.2, 4.3	4.3, 4.4	4.5	5.2
Fair trade	4.4	5.5	5.5			
Gender and equality / Role of women	5.2		1.5, 5.4	3.6, 5.2	5.3	5.4
Interfaith	4.3	5.6	5.6	2.2, 5.6	5.5	5.6
Medical ethics	3.6	4.2	4.2	5.4	4.1	4.4, 4.5
Relationships / Marriage / Family	5.2	5.2, 5.3	3.3, 5.3	5.2, 5.3	5.1, 5.2	4.6
Science and religion	4.5	4.1		4.6, 5.4		4.3
Secular and atheist worldviews	4.5		1.1, 1.6	5.5	4.4, 5.5	4.3
War and peace	4.2, 5.5, 5.6	4.5, 4.6	3.1, 4.2, 5.5	4.3	5.5	5.2, 5.5
Wealth / Poverty / Charity	5.3	5.1, 5.6	3.1, 5.1	3.2	5.4	3.6, 3.8, 4.1

Introduction to *Living Faiths*

How we live now

Living Faiths draws on the rich heritage of culture and diversity in twenty-first century Britain. The series focuses on case studies (shown through film and print) of young people and their families in the UK who describe how their faith affects the way they live and the moral and ethical decisions they make. The emphasis is on the personal significance of religious faith, exploring the question: What does it *mean* to be a Buddhist, Christian, Hindu, Jew, Muslim or Sikh?

This approach allows students to experience the subject fully and see its relevance to their own lives. Engagement with the case study families creates awareness of diversity, encouraging respect and enhancing social awareness. Hearing and seeing young people sharing their faith and aspects of their daily lives helps students clarify their own perspectives and reflect on their experiences, build their sense of identity and belonging, challenge prejudices and provide the knowledge and understanding to enable them to flourish in their communities.

Flexible and adaptable

Living Faiths is a series of six books, teacher guides and online resources covering Buddhism, Christianity, Hinduism, Islam, Judaism, and Sikhism. The series is designed to allow teachers the flexibility to teach by faiths or by themes, and the Scheme of Work (on page 3) provides guidance at a glance on how to teach by themes. Through structured questioning and activities, students are encouraged to make links as they learn about a range of faiths and secular world views. They are expected to identify similarities and differences within faiths, and the *Teacher Guide* further provides suggestions on how to compare and contrast between faiths. There is a strong emphasis on sources including sacred texts, film interviews, audio and music to give students access to the lived experience of the case study families and learn what their faith means in practice.

Pedagogy

The series takes a mixed pedagogical approach inspired by the important ethnographic work that has been developed in RE in recent years. Throughout the series students are introduced to the study of faith as it is practised by believers today. The enquiry-driven focus enables them to engage with the voices and personalities of faith, getting beyond generalizations and over-simplifications, to enter into dialogue with people about their faith. Through this dialogue with living faith students will be encouraged to reflect on the experiences and beliefs of others and also on their own experiences of faith, belief and what really matters in life.

The *Living Faiths* series has been designed to engage, interest and challenge students. Each unit has an intriguing title, often a question, to capture the interest of students as soon as the lesson begins. The 'starter' activities get students thinking and discussing, drawing on their prior learning or their personal experiences as ways into the main lesson focus.

Questioning

Questioning is fundamental to good teaching and learning. Higher order questions enable students to tackle issues at a deep level and extend their thinking, develop independence in the way they learn and think and come to a fuller understanding of an idea because they have tried to explain it themselves. Bloom's Taxonomy (1956), is a useful tool for planning sequences of different types of questions of increasing difficulty to promote higher order thinking. Many of the activities are designed for pair and group discussion or for independent and small group research to promote student participation. Through the activities students will develop the ability to speculate, to raise their own questions and seek answers for themselves.

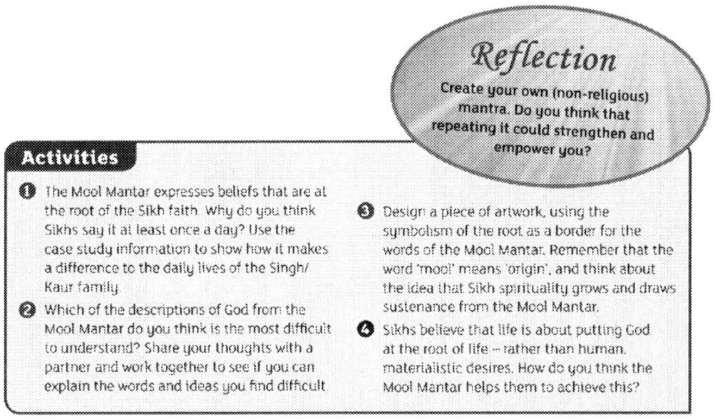
Reflection

Create your own (non-religious) mantra. Do you think that repeating it could strengthen and empower you?

Activities

1. The Mool Mantar expresses beliefs that are at the root of the Sikh faith. Why do you think Sikhs say it at least once a day? Use the case study information to show how it makes a difference to the daily lives of the Singh/Kaur family.
2. Which of the descriptions of God from the Mool Mantar do you think is the most difficult to understand? Share your thoughts with a partner and work together to see if you can explain the words and ideas you find difficult.
3. Design a piece of artwork, using the symbolism of the root as a border for the words of the Mool Mantar. Remember that the word 'mool' means 'origin', and think about the idea that Sikh spirituality grows and draws sustenance from the Mool Mantar.
4. Sikhs believe that life is about putting God at the root of life – rather than human, materialistic desires. How do you think the Mool Mantar helps them to achieve this?

The activities are colour coded to identify three modes of thinking that are particularly valuable in the study of religion, philosophy and the broad area of social sciences.

Students are encouraged to:

- **Red: 'Think like a theologian'** these questions focus on understanding the nature of religious belief, its symbolism and spiritual significance; in the *Student Book* they are highlighted by a red question number
- **Blue: 'Think like a philosopher'** these questions focus on analysing and debating big ideas such as truth and reality; in the *Student Book* they are highlighted by a blue question number
- **Green: 'Think like a social scientist'** these questions focus on exploring and analysing why people do what they do and how belief affects action; in the *Student Book* they are highlighted by a green question number

Reflection

Reflection helps students to deepen their thinking and apply their learning about the religious beliefs and practices of others. It encourages them to explore their own beliefs in the light of what they learn, whether they are religious or not, and how they impact on personal ethics.

Thinking skills

In RE students are expected to think in increasing depth about complex issues to do with faith, beliefs, ideas and motivation. Philosophical enquiry-based approaches such as mind-mapping help students to think creatively, analytically and critically; to listen to, evaluate and respond to the views and ideas of others; to give reasons for their opinions, make connections and hypothesize; to give both sides of an argument, evaluate and draw conclusions.

Assessment

At the end of each unit there is a final assessment task which draws together students' learning.

Assessment for learning strategies are built into every unit:

- Learning objectives for each unit are written in student-friendly language and shared with students
- Students know what standards and levels they are aiming for
- Self- and peer-assessment opportunities are supported by 'I can' statements
- **AT1 Learning *about* religion** is assessed using auto-marked tests to help save you time setting questions and marking
- **AT2 Learning *from* religion** is assessed with step-by-step tasks and support materials. These use effective assessment for learning strategies to help students recognize next steps and improve performance.

We hope that you will enjoy using this series to bring real families of faith into the classroom, and to introduce students to the liveliness and relevance of religious education.

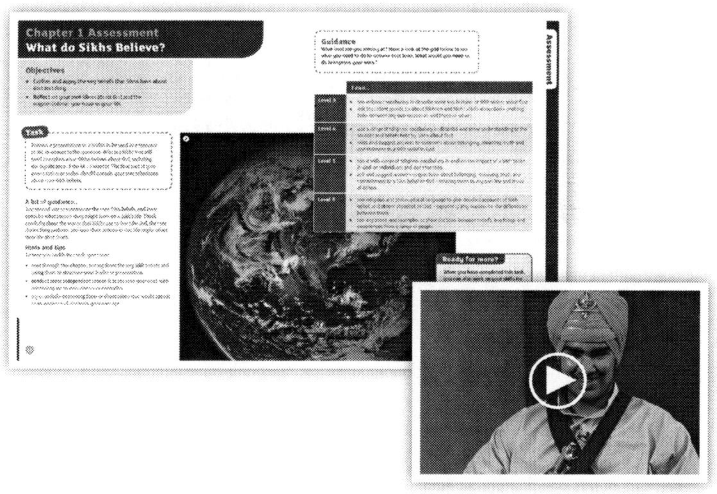

Janet Dyson
(Series Editor)

Robert Bowie
(Series Consultant)

About this Series

Living Faiths Sikhism is one of six Religious Education Student Books covering the following major faiths: Buddhism, Christianity, Hinduism, Islam, Judaism, and Sikhism. This series fully integrates real-life film clips and other exciting multimedia resources on the *Oxbox Online* with the *Student Books* and *Teacher Guides*, so your lessons can be delivered easily and seamlessly.

The series components

The series consist of:

For students

- Six *Student Books* (and/or six *Online Student Books*)
- Six *OxBox Online* Lessons, Resources and Assessments.

For teachers

- Six *Teacher Guides*
- Six *OxBox Online* Lessons, Resources and Assessments (includes teacher access to the accompanying *Online Student Book*).

Student Book

The ***Living Faiths Sikhism Student Book*** uses **real-life case studies** to encourage students to ask questions, actively engage with **moral** and **ethical** issues, and reflect on the relevance of RE.

Starter activities spark your students' interest in new topics

The 'Reflection' feature helps your students to consider beliefs and practices of others, and how they link to their own lives and beliefs

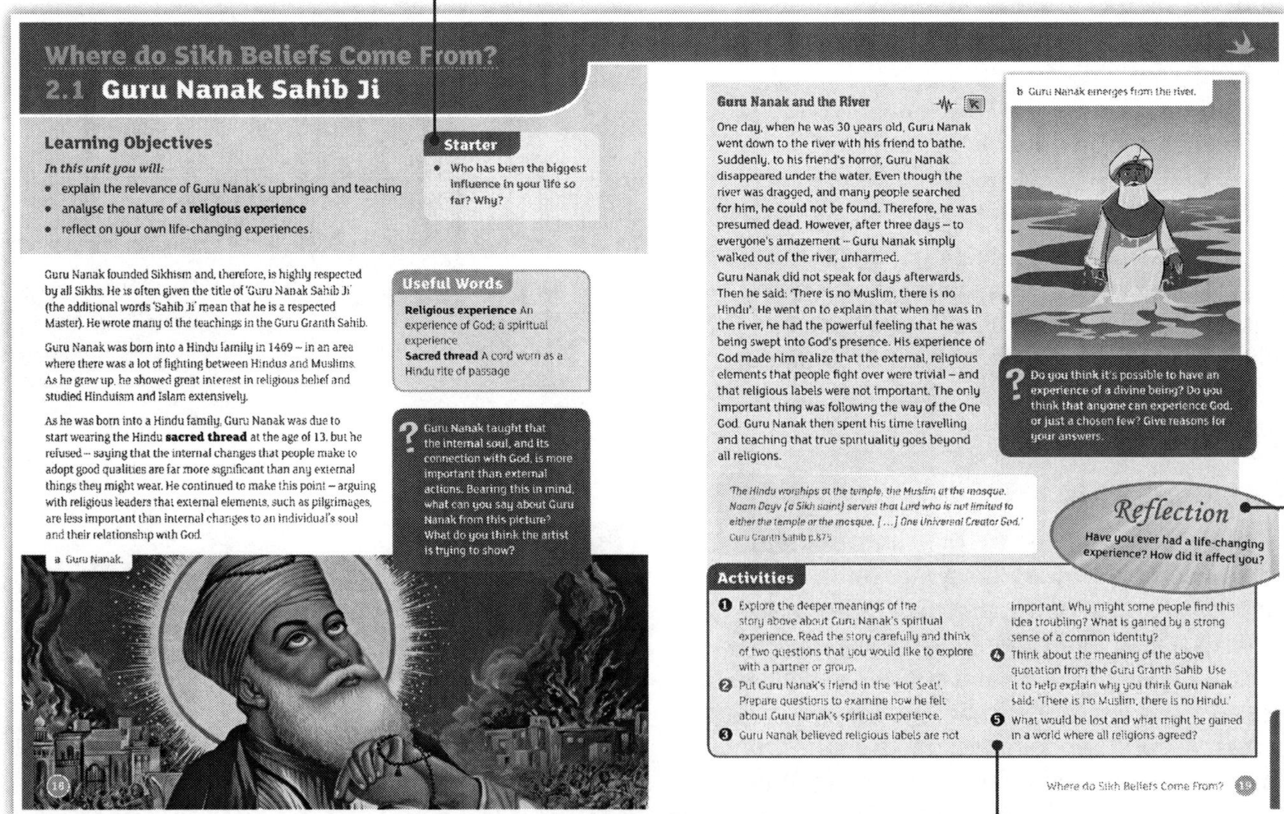

Where do Sikh Beliefs Come From?

2.1 Guru Nanak Sahib Ji

Learning Objectives

In this unit you will:

- explain the relevance of Guru Nanak's upbringing and teaching
- analyse the nature of a **religious experience**
- reflect on your own life-changing experiences

Starter

- Who has been the biggest influence in your life so far? Why?

Guru Nanak founded Sikhism and, therefore, is highly respected by all Sikhs. He is often given the title of 'Guru Nanak Sahib Ji' (the additional words 'Sahib Ji' mean that he is a respected Master). He wrote many of the teachings in the Guru Granth Sahib.

Guru Nanak was born into a Hindu family in 1469 – in an area where there was a lot of fighting between Hindus and Muslims. As he grew up, he showed great interest in religious belief and studied Hinduism and Islam extensively.

As he was born into a Hindu family, Guru Nanak was due to start wearing the Hindu **sacred thread** at the age of 13, but he refused – saying that the internal changes that people make to adopt good qualities are far more significant than any external things they might wear. He continued to make this point – arguing with religious leaders that external elements, such as pilgrimages, are less important than internal changes to an individual's soul and their relationship with God.

Useful Words

Religious experience An experience of God: a spiritual experience

Sacred thread A cord worn as a Hindu rite of passage

? Guru Nanak taught that the internal soul, and its connection with God, is more important than external actions. Bearing this in mind, what can you say about Guru Nanak from this picture? What do you think the artist is trying to show?

a Guru Nanak.

18

Guru Nanak and the River

One day, when he was 30 years old, Guru Nanak went down to the river with his friend to bathe. Suddenly, to his friend's horror, Guru Nanak disappeared under the water. Even though the river was dragged, and many people searched for him, he could not be found. Therefore, he was presumed dead. However, after three days – to everyone's amazement – Guru Nanak simply walked out of the river, unharmed.

Guru Nanak did not speak for days afterwards. Then he said: 'There is no Muslim, there is no Hindu'. He went on to explain that when he was in the river, he had the powerful feeling that he was being swept into God's presence. His experience of God made him realize that the external, religious elements that people fight over were trivial – and that religious labels were not important. The only important thing was following the way of the One God. Guru Nanak then spent his time travelling and teaching that true spirituality goes beyond all religions.

b Guru Nanak emerges from the river.

? Do you think it's possible to have an experience of a divine being? Do you think that anyone can experience God, or just a chosen few? Give reasons for your answers.

'The Hindu worships at the temple, the Muslim at the mosque. Naam Dayv (a Sikh saint) serves that Lord who is not limited to either the temple or the mosque. [...] One Universal Creator God.'
Guru Granth Sahib p.875

Reflection

Have you ever had a life-changing experience? How did it affect you?

Activities

1. Explore the deeper meanings of the story above about Guru Nanak's spiritual experience. Read the story carefully and think of two questions that you would like to explore with a partner or group.
2. Put Guru Nanak's friend in the 'Hot Seat'. Prepare questions to examine how he felt about Guru Nanak's spiritual experience.
3. Guru Nanak believed religious labels are not important. Why might some people find this idea troubling? What is gained by a strong sense of a common identity?
4. Think about the meaning of the above quotation from the Guru Granth Sahib. Use it to help explain why you think Guru Nanak said: 'There is no Muslim, there is no Hindu.'
5. What would be lost and what might be gained in a world where all religions agreed?

Where do Sikh Beliefs Come From? 19

Sikhism Student Book

Colour-coded activities develop varied skills and are structured to encourage progression and allow differentiation

Case studies provide first-hand experience of real Sikh families talking about their faith

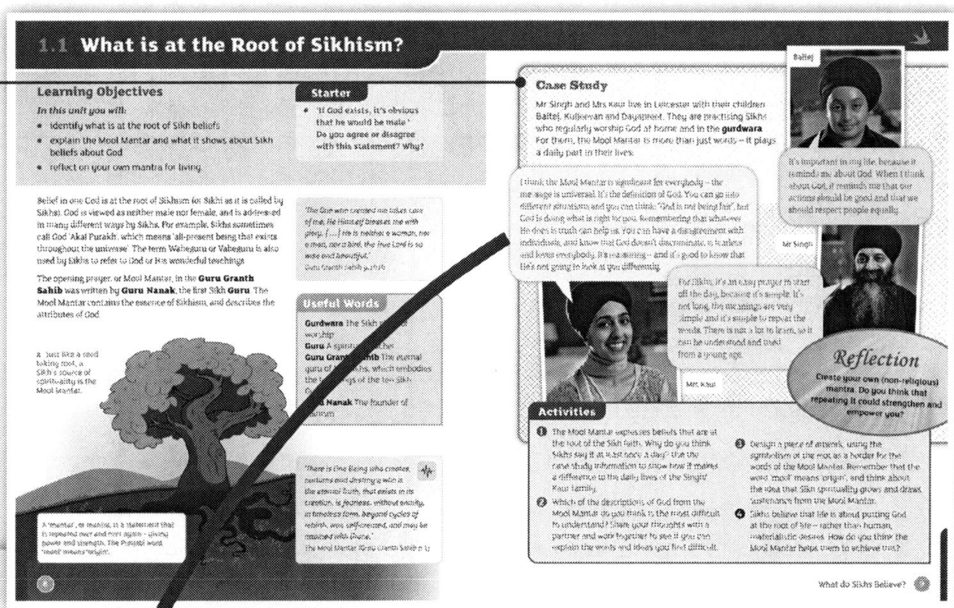

Sikhism Student Book

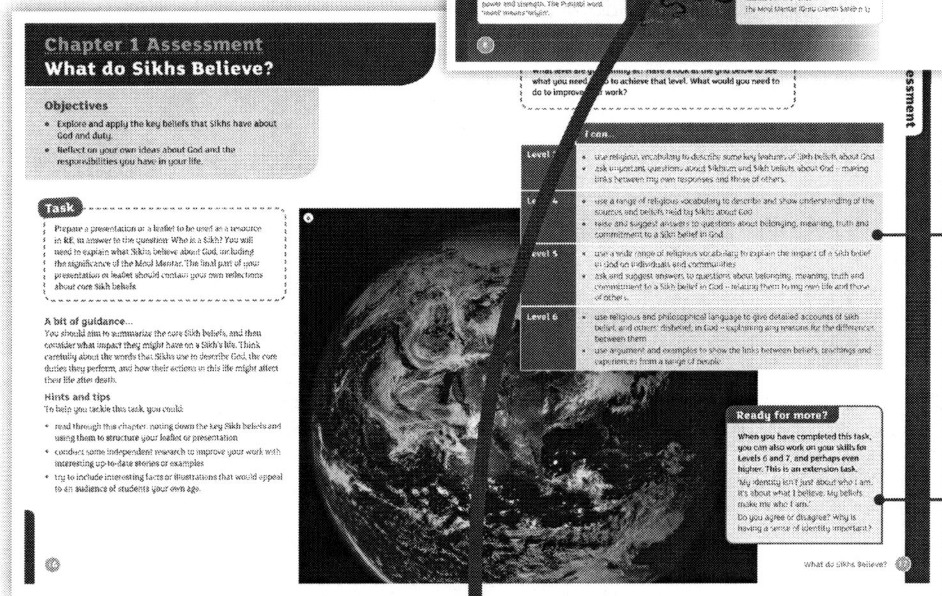

There is an assessment spread for every chapter in the *Student Book* to help students determine what level they are aiming for and make progress

Extension tasks within assessments challenge more able students

Case studies are linked directly to films on the *OxBox Online* and are marked with film icons on each page

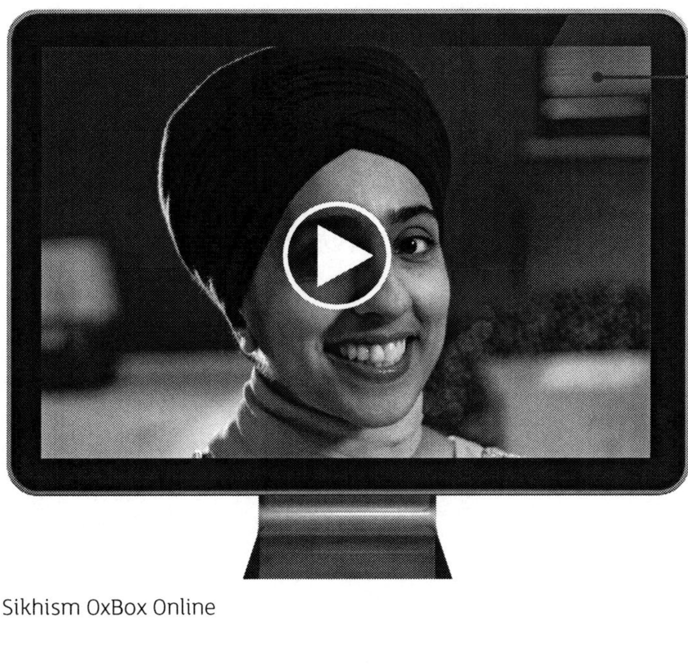

Sikhism OxBox Online

Authors

Experienced RE Consultant **Janet Dyson** and well-known author and PGCE tutor **Robert Bowie** lead the author **Julie Haigh**, who is an experienced RE teacher.

Using this Book

Teacher Guide

The ***Living Faiths Sikhism Teacher Guide*** aims to save you time and effort. It provides **full support** and guidance for the *Sikhism Student Book*, including **practical tasks** and **creative suggestions** for incorporating differentiation into your teaching.

What it provides

For each chapter of the student book, this book provides:

- a chapter overview
- help at a glance for each unit
- further suggestions for class and homework
- an assessment overview.

It also has a **Glossary** at the back, covering the RE terms students will meet.

Please turn to the **Contents List** on page 2 to see how this book is structured. While the Living Faiths series is organized by religion, a **Scheme of Work** on page 3 is also provided to help you teach RE **by themes**.

Find out more about the four main components below.

The chapter overview

This is your introduction to the corresponding *Student Book* chapter.

Shows how the *Student Book* chapter relates to the KS3 RE Programme of Study (non-statutory)

Reminds you that some lessons, including starters and plenaries, will need resources prepared in advance

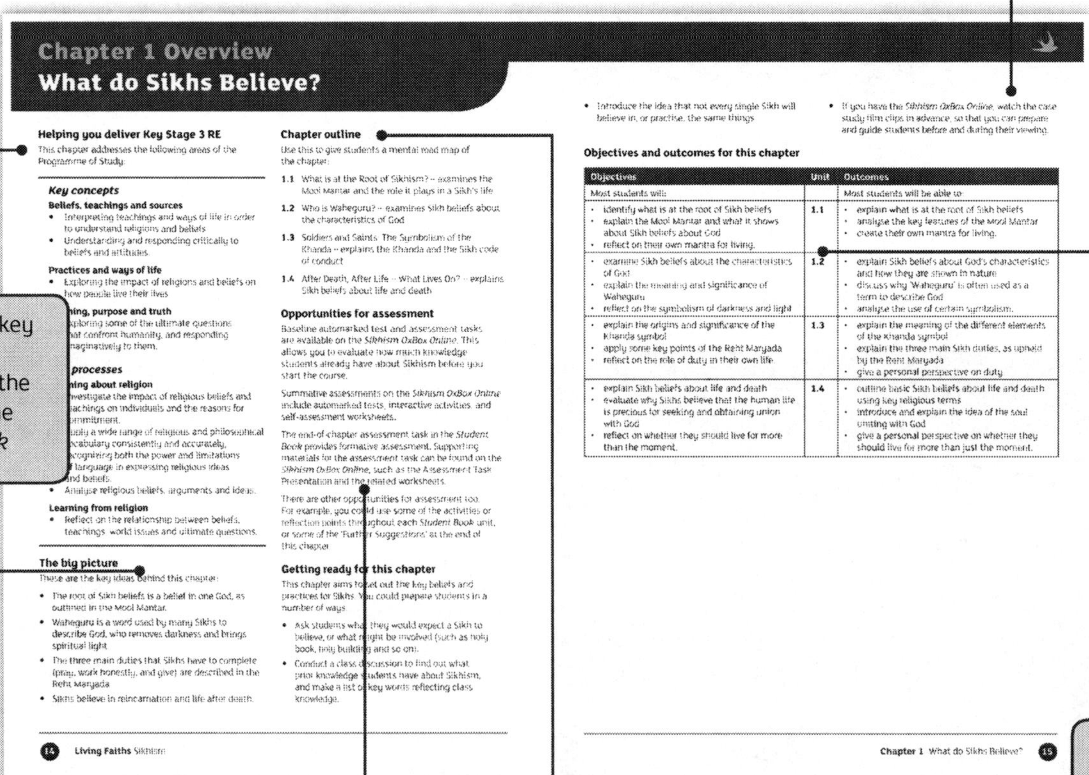

Sets out the key ideas within, and behind, the chapter in the *Student Book*

Sets out the objectives and outcomes for the chapter, and the corresponding unit numbers

Points you to the assessment material for the chapter (summative and formal assessments, and related resources)

Gives a brief summary of what's covered in the *Student Book* chapter. It will help you give students a road map for the chapter

Help at a glance for each unit

These pages give comprehensive help for each unit of the *Student Book*.

Summarizes ideas covered in the unit, plus underlying ideas where appropriate

Starts with a brief walk through the unit, to show you how it develops

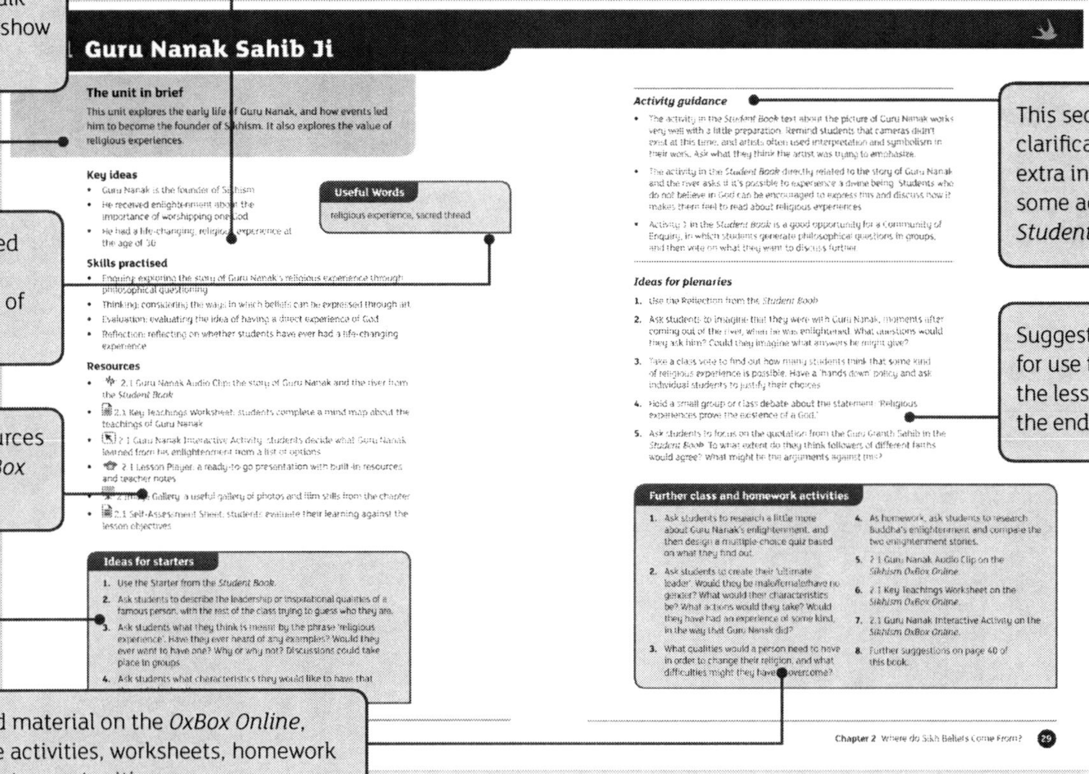

This section provides clarification and extra information for some activities in the *Student Book*

New terms introduced in the unit. See the glossary at the back of the book

Suggests plenaries for use throughout the lesson, not just at the end

A list of all the resources available on the *OxBox Online* for the unit

Suggestions for starters

Points you to related material on the *OxBox Online*, including interactive activities, worksheets, homework ideas and assessment opportunities

Further suggestions for class and homework

These pages give a bank of further suggestions for class and homework.

They have been graded *, ** or *** according to level of difficulty.

These suggestions are addressed directly to students.

1.1 What is at the Root of Sikhism?

1 If you were to put one person at the centre of your life – famous or not, alive or dead – who would it be and why? Think carefully about how you explain your choice, because this is an important skill. *

1.3 Soldiers and Saints: The Symbolism of the Khanda

1 Pray, work honestly, and give are the three main duties laid out in the Reht Maryada. Choose one of the three and create a flier that explains why it should apply to everyone, from the Sikh point of view. **

Suggestions are graded, but some are suitable for all levels, and differentiated by outcome

The assessment overview

This section introduces you to the end-of-chapter assessment task from the *Student Book*, and describes the support materials available for the chapter.

Assessment in the *Student Book*

You will find an assessment task at the end of every chapter which focuses on AT2. In this chapter, the task asks students to prepare a presentation or a leaflet to be used as a resource in RE, in answer to the question: Who is a Sikh?

In the *Student Book* (and on the supporting worksheets), you'll find guidance about levels of assessment that you can use to help your students understand what their work should include. You could ask them to use these criteria for self- or peer-assessment once they've completed the task.

Living Faiths Assessment

Student Book

- Assessment Task
- Levels Guidance

OxBox Online

- Auto-Marked Test
- Assessment Task Presentation
- Assessment Worksheets

The purpose of the end-of-chapter assessment task from the *Student Book* is summarized

You can see all the assessment materials available for the chapter at a glance

OxBox Online

Living Faiths Sikhism OxBox Online is packed full of guided support and ideas for running and creating effective lessons on Sikhism. It's intuitive to use, customizable, and can be accessed online.

It consists of:

- Sikhism Lessons, Resources and Assessments (includes teacher access to the accompanying *Online Student Book*)
- *Sikhism Online Student Book*.

Lessons, Resources and Assessment

Living Faiths Sikhism OxBox Online – Lessons, Resources and Assessment provides over one hundred lively built-in resources, including unique specially commissioned films of real Sikh families practising their faiths, interactive activities, ready-to-go lesson presentations, and supported assessment tasks.
You can even **adapt** many of these resources to suit you and your students' individual needs, and **upload** your existing resources so everything can be accessed from one location. Image collections and audio clips are also included to help bring RE to life in your classroom.

Lessons, Resources and Assessment provides:

- Resources
- Lessons
- Assessment and Markbook
- Teacher access to the *Online Student Book*.

Find out more about the four main components below.

Resources
Click on the **Resources tab** at the top of the screen to access the full list of *Living Faiths Sikhism* resources.

The Resources section has more than:

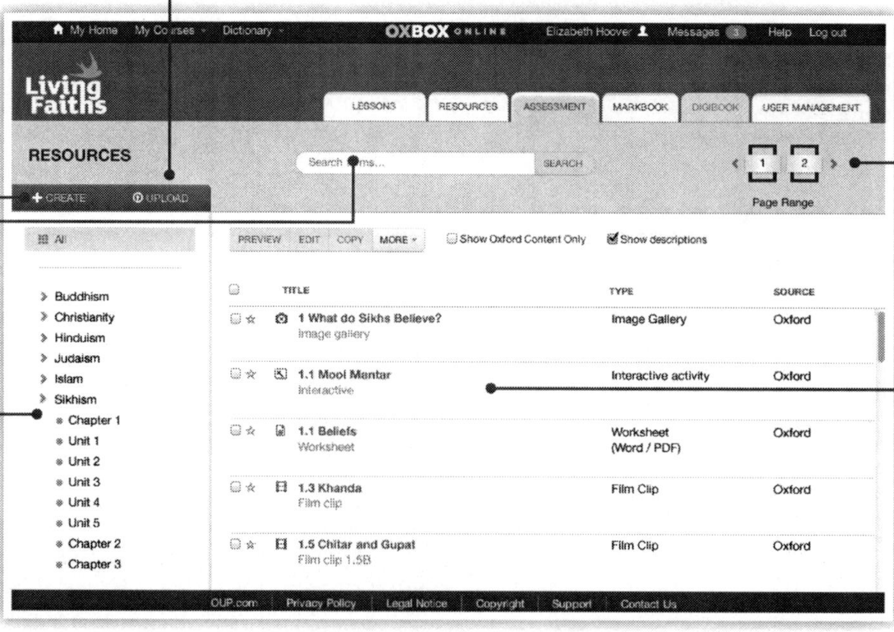

Sikhism OxBox Online

The Resources section has more than:

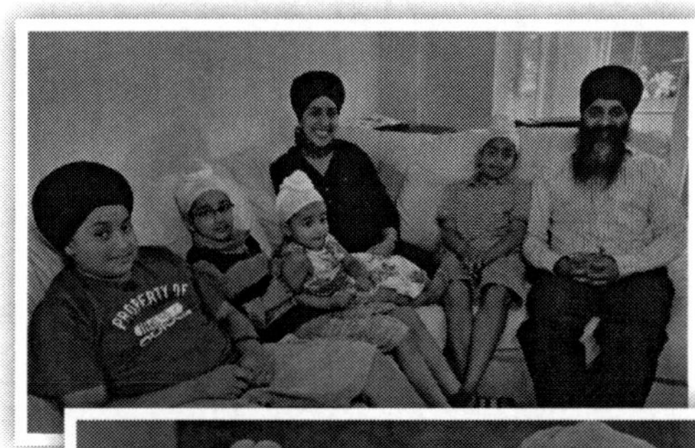

20 Film clips: Specially commissioned films help your students to actively engage with RE through watching real Sikh families practise their faith and to explore the diversity within Sikhism.

10 Audio clips: Specially commissioned music and narrated sources help bring RE alive in your classroom.

70 Worksheets: Creative worksheets that help provide differentiation/extension material for each unit, and film worksheets to help students assess their own learning of the case study film clips and link ideas back to the *Student Book* unit. They are provided as PDFs, which you can print off and photocopy, and as Word files, which you can amend to suit your students' needs.

30 Interactive activities: Various types of activities are available for each unit as short main activities, plenaries or summative assessments. They can also be used for independent study. Most of these activities are auto-marked to help you save time marking.

80 Images: An image gallery with captions is provided for each chapter so you can easily enlarge any photo or artwork from the *Student Book* on screen and use it as a discussion starter, use them in your own worksheets, or give them to students to use in class or homework activities.

OxBox Online **resources are fully integrated with the** ***Student Book*****:**

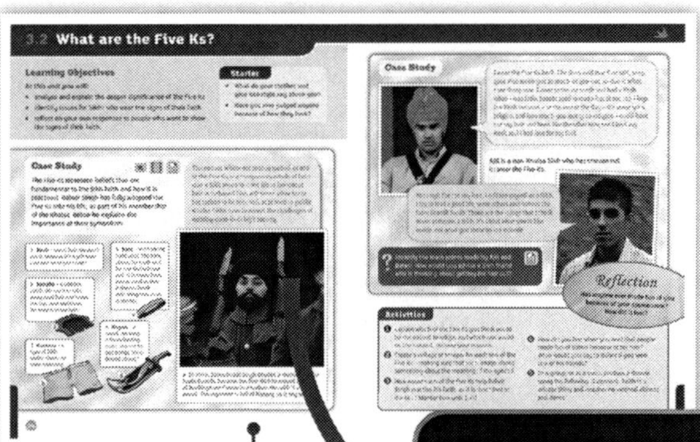

Sikhism Student Book

Use the accompanying film worksheets to help your students consolidate what they have learnt

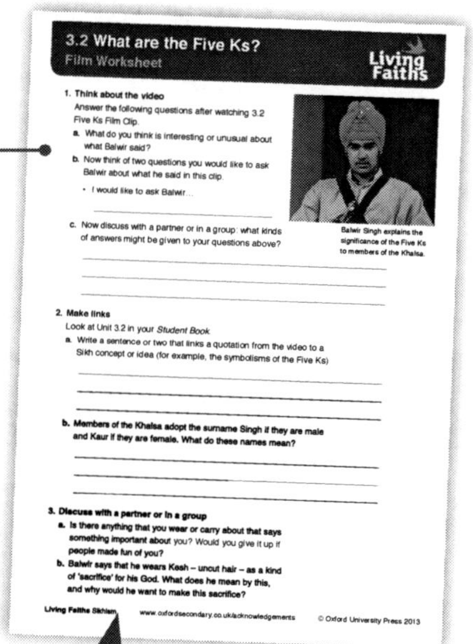

3.2 What are the Five Ks?
Film Worksheet

1. Think about the video
Answer the following questions after watching 3.2 Five Ks Film Clip.
a. What do you think is interesting or unusual about what Balwir said?
b. Now think of two questions you would like to ask Balwir about what he said in this clip.
• I would like to ask Balwir...
c. Now discuss with a partner or in a group: what kinds of answers might be given to your questions above?

Balwir Singh explains the significance of the Five Ks to members of the Khalsa.

2. Make links
Look at Unit 3.2 in your *Student Book*
a. Write a sentence or two that links a quotation from the video to a Sikh concept or idea (for example, the symbolisms of the Five Ks)
b. Members of the Khalsa adopt the surname Singh if they are male and Kaur if they are female. What do these names mean?

3. Discuss with a partner or in a group
a. Is there anything that you wear or carry about that says something important about you? Would you give it up if people made fun of you?
b. Balwir says that he wears Kesh – uncut hair – as a kind of 'sacrifice' for his God. What does he mean by this, and why would he want to make this sacrifice?

Living Faiths Sikhism www.oxfordsecondary.co.uk/acknowledgements © Oxford University Press 2013

Real Sikh families are featured in the *Student Book* and you can find the specially commissioned films related to *Student Book* units on *OxBox Online*

All the resources and assessments are **fully integrated** with the *Sikhism Student Book*

OxBox Online

Lesson presentations

Click on the **Lessons tab** to access the full list of *Living Faiths Sikhism* lessons and notes.

Ready-to-play lesson presentations complement every unit in the book. Each lesson presentation is easy to launch, and features unit objectives, the related starters, worksheets, film and interactive resources, and closes with a plenary activity or reflection. You can further **personalize** the lessons by adding in your own resources and notes. Your lessons and notes can be accessed by your whole department, and they are a great time-saver and **ideal for non-specialist** teachers and cover lessons.

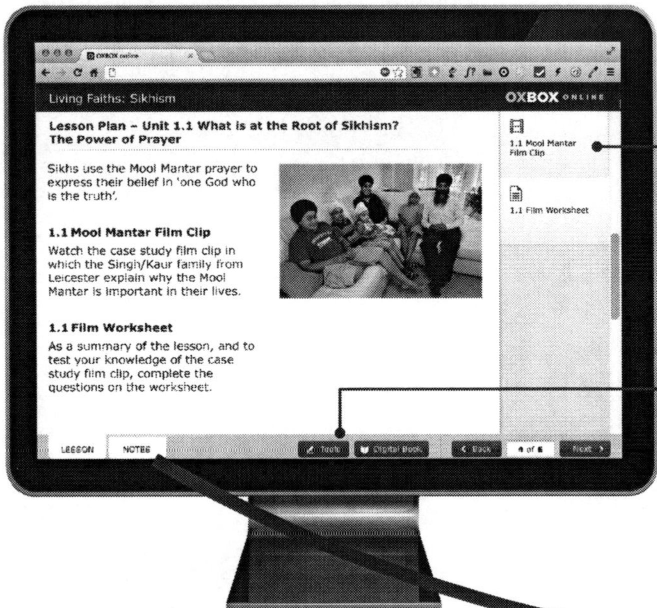

Resources are built into each lesson presentation so all the relevant activities, film clips and worksheets are ready to launch

The resources you want to use can also be rearranged and launched in sequence to suit your classroom needs

Every lesson is accompanied by teacher notes to fully support your lesson delivery

Slide 2

Film clip: Students watch 1.1 Mool Mantar Film Clip in which the Singh/Kaur family from Leicester explain why the Mool Mantar is important in their lives.

Activity guidance: The case study film clip can be used to develop the students' understanding of the Mool Mantar and its central place in Sikhism.

Worksheet: 1.1 Film Worksheet allows students to assess their understanding of the case study film clip by linking ideas to the *Student Book*.

Activity guidance: You might like to extend students' understanding of the concepts discussed in the film clip by asking them to complete the accompanying worksheet after viewing. It might be useful to present the worksheet to students in advance, so that they have the questions in mind as they watch the films. Responses to questions that prompt pair or group discussion could be shared with the class at the end of the exercise.

Extension: Ask students to create a word cloud that is all about the Mool Mantar, but doesn't include any of the key words from it. They should think about what the key words mean and choose ones that mean the same to go into the word cloud.

Assessment and Markbook

Click on the **Assessment tab** to find a wide range of assessment materials to help you deliver a varied, motivating, and effective assessment programme.

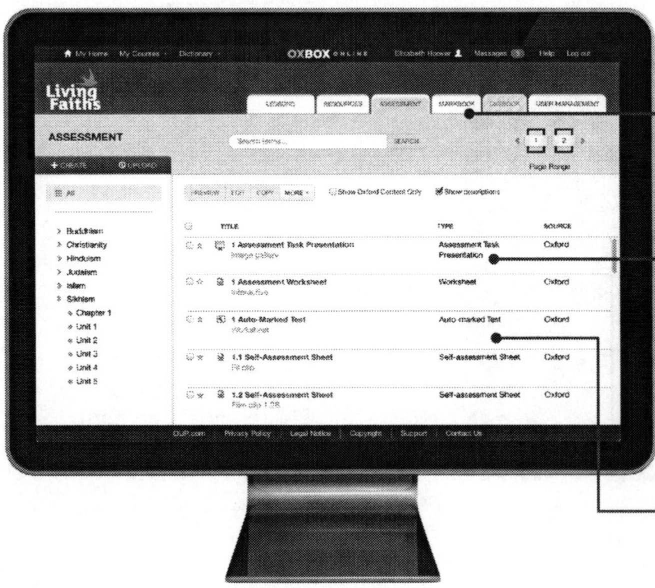

A markbook and reporting function help keep everything you need in one place

Learning from religion (AT2) is assessed with step-by-step tasks and support materials

Learning about religion (AT1) is assessed using auto-marked tests to help save you time

The Assessment section provides:

- **2 baseline tests:** These tests cover both **Attainment Target 1** (learning *about* religion) and **Attainment Target 2** (learning *from* religion), and they can help you to quickly assess the prior RE knowledge that your new KS3 students may have.
- **5 auto-marked tests**: Each end-of-chapter auto-marked test assesses **AT1**. The marks are automatically reported in the **Markbook tab**.
- **30 self-assessment worksheets**: Self-assessment worksheets help students to self- or peer-evaluate the skills they have learnt from each unit.
- **5 assessment task presentations**: Each end-of-chapter assessment task in the *Student Book*, which assesses **AT2**, has a front-of-class presentation for you to use to help guide students towards understanding and analysing what the question/task is asking of them. You can lead students through this step-by-step presentation and help them decide how to prepare to answer the question.
- **15 assessment worksheets**: These worksheets complement the assessment tasks in the *Student Book* and the assessment task presentations. They recap the task, provide a self-evaluation chart, and space for students to prepare their work.

A **Markbook** with reporting function completes the *OxBox Online* assessment package, so you can keep track of all your students' test results and assessment scores. This includes both the auto-marked tests and work that need to be marked by you. It is also easy to import class registers and create user accounts for all your students.

Online Student Book

The ***Sikhism Online Student Book*** provides you with an on-screen version of the *Student Book* for you to use on your whiteboard with the whole class.

Teacher access to the *Online Student Book* is **automatically available** as part of the Lessons, Resources and Assessment package. You can also choose to buy access for your students.

Both teacher and student access include a simple bank of tools so you can personalize the book and take notes.

It can be accessed on other devices, such as tablets.

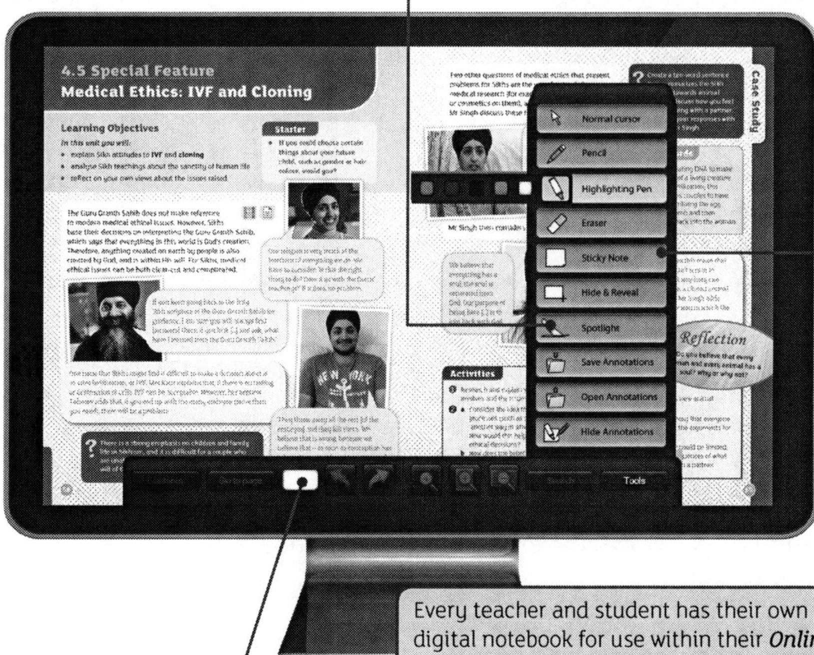

Chapter 1 Overview
What do Sikhs Believe?

Helping you deliver Key Stage 3 RE

This chapter addresses the following areas of the Programme of Study:

Key concepts

Beliefs, teachings and sources

- Interpreting teachings and ways of life in order to understand religions and beliefs.
- Understanding and responding critically to beliefs and attitudes.

Practices and ways of life

- Exploring the impact of religions and beliefs on how people live their lives.

Meaning, purpose and truth

- Exploring some of the ultimate questions that confront humanity, and responding imaginatively to them.

Key processes

Learning about religion

- Investigate the impact of religious beliefs and teachings on individuals and the reasons for commitment.
- Apply a wide range of religious and philosophical vocabulary consistently and accurately, recognizing both the power and limitations of language in expressing religious ideas and beliefs.
- Analyse religious beliefs, arguments and ideas.

Learning from religion

- Reflect on the relationship between beliefs, teachings, world issues and ultimate questions.

The big picture

These are the key ideas behind this chapter:

- The root of Sikh beliefs is a belief in one God, as outlined in the Mool Mantar.
- Waheguru is a word used by many Sikhs to describe God, who removes darkness and brings spiritual light.
- The three main duties that Sikhs have to complete (pray, work honestly, and give) are described in the Reht Maryada.
- Sikhs believe in reincarnation and life after death.

Chapter outline

Use this to give students a mental road map of the chapter:

1.1 What is at the Root of Sikhism? – examines the Mool Mantar and the role it plays in a Sikh's life

1.2 Who is Waheguru? – examines Sikh beliefs about the characteristics of God

1.3 Soldiers and Saints: The Symbolism of the Khanda – explains the Khanda and the Sikh code of conduct

1.4 After Death, After Life – What Lives On? – explains Sikh beliefs about life and death

Opportunities for assessment

Baseline automarked test and assessment tasks are available on the *Sikhism OxBox Online*. This allows you to evaluate how much knowledge students already have about Sikhism before you start the course.

Summative assessments on the *Sikhism OxBox Online* include automarked tests, interactive activities, and self-assessment worksheets.

The end-of-chapter assessment task in the *Student Book* provides formative assessment. Supporting materials for the assessment task can be found on the *Sikhism OxBox Online*, such as the Assessment Task Presentation and the related worksheets.

There are other opportunities for assessment too. For example, you could use some of the activities or reflection points throughout each *Student Book* unit, or some of the 'Further Suggestions' at the end of this chapter.

Getting ready for this chapter

This chapter aims to set out the key beliefs and practices for Sikhs. You could prepare students in a number of ways:

- Ask students what they would expect a Sikh to believe, or what might be involved (such as holy book, holy building and so on).
- Conduct a class discussion to find out what prior knowledge students have about Sikhism, and make a list of key words reflecting class knowledge.

- Introduce the idea that not every single Sikh will believe in, or practise, the same things.
- If you have the *Sikhism OxBox Online*, watch the case study film clips in advance, so that you can prepare and guide students before and during their viewing.

Objectives and outcomes for this chapter

Objectives	Unit	Outcomes
Most students will:		Most students will be able to:
• identify what is at the root of Sikh beliefs • explain the Mool Mantar and what it shows about Sikh beliefs about God • reflect on their own mantra for living.	**1.1**	• explain what is at the root of Sikh beliefs • analyse the key features of the Mool Mantar • create their own mantra for living.
• examine Sikh beliefs about the characteristics of God • explain the meaning and significance of Waheguru • reflect on the symbolism of darkness and light.	**1.2**	• explain Sikh beliefs about God's characteristics and how they are shown in nature • discuss why 'Waheguru' is often used as a term to describe God • analyse the use of certain symbolism.
• explain the origins and significance of the Khanda symbol • apply some key points of the Reht Maryada • reflect on the role of duty in their own life.	**1.3**	• explain the meaning of the different elements of the Khanda symbol • explain the three main Sikh duties, as upheld by the Reht Maryada • give a personal perspective on duty.
• explain Sikh beliefs about life and death • evaluate why Sikhs believe that the human life is precious for seeking and obtaining union with God • reflect on whether they should live for more than the moment.	**1.4**	• outline basic Sikh beliefs about life and death using key religious terms • introduce and explain the idea of the soul uniting with God • give a personal perspective on whether they should live for more than just the moment.

1.1 What is at the Root of Sikhism?

The unit in brief

The unit looks at the Mool Mantar, which is the opening prayer of the Guru Granth Sahib written by the first Sikh Guru, Guru Nanak. Members of a case study family explain the core beliefs that it contains and why they are so central to Sikhism.

Key ideas

- The Mool Mantar contains core beliefs for Sikhs, and is spoken daily
- God is described in the Mool Mantar as being 'One' and the 'Creator'
- Sikhs regularly state their beliefs, so they are reminded to involve God in their day-to-day lives

Useful Words

Gurdwara, Guru, Guru Granth Sahib, Guru Nanak

Skills practised

- Literacy: interpreting the key words and ideas in scripture
- Application: applying core beliefs to the practices of a Sikh family
- Thinking: considering how beliefs may impact a person's life
- Reflection: creating and reflecting on a personal mantra

Resources

- 1.1 Mool Mantar Audio Clip: a recording of the Mool Mantar
- 1.1 Mool Mantar Film Clip: the Singh/Kaur family from Leicester explain why the Mool Mantar is important in their lives
- 1.1 Film Worksheet: students assess their understanding of the case study film clip by linking ideas to the *Student Book*
- 1.1 Mool Mantar Interactive Activity: students select sentences that correctly describe the Mool Mantar
- 1.1 Lesson Player: a ready-to-go presentation with built-in resources and teacher notes
- 1 Image Gallery: a useful gallery of photos and film stills from the chapter
- 1.1 Self-Assessment Sheet: students evaluate their learning against the lesson objectives

Ideas for starters

1. Use the Starter from the *Student Book*.
2. Take suggestions from the class to create a mind-map on the board containing as many key words or ideas as students can come up with that they think are linked to Sikhism. Discuss them, even if they are wrong, to deal with any misconceptions.
3. Find and show a selection of images related to Sikhism (or use 1 Image Gallery on the *Sikhism OxBox Online*) and see if students can identify any of them and put them into context.
4. Ask students to write down three things they know about Sikhs – one thing they're sure of, and two things they think they know are true.

Activity guidance

- For the starter activities, you may wish to get mini whiteboards or large pieces of paper and get students to note down their ideas. They could then compare and contrast their ideas with others before formulating a final response to the class.
- Activity 3 in the *Student Book* provides a good opportunity for peer assessment. In pairs, students could provide positive and constructive feedback, based on how well their partners have identified key Sikh beliefs.

Ideas for plenaries

1. Use the Reflection from the *Student Book*.
2. Ask students to revisit their initial starter ideas. What do they know now that they didn't know at the start?
3. Ask students what they can tell about Sikh beliefs by looking at the Mool Mantar. Ask them to make a list of any other things that they expect Sikhs to believe as a result of reading the Mool Mantar.

Further class and homework activities

1. Use 1.1 Mool Mantar Interactive Activity on the *Sikhism OxBox Online* to consolidate students' learning about the meaning and purpose of the Mool Mantar.
2. 1.1 Mool Mantar Film Clip on the *Sikhism OxBox Online*.
3. 1.1 Film Worksheet on the *Sikhism OxBox Online*.
4. Play 1.1 Audio Clip on the *Sikhism OxBox Online*, and ask students to explain how it made them feel. Were there any words or phrases that confused them? Can they explain why Sikhs might draw comfort from repeating those words?
5. Further suggestions on page 24 of this book.

1.2 Who is Waheguru?

The unit in brief

This unit explores the meaning of the word 'Waheguru', how it is used and how Sikhs meditate on its significance. Students are encouraged to reflect on the concept of light and darkness, relating it to the world around them and their own lives.

Key ideas

- 'Waheguru' means 'Wonderful Lord' and is used by Sikhs to refer to God
- 'Waheguru' is used in Sikh worship and meditation
- Sikhs believe that Waheguru is the one who removes darkness and brings light

Useful Word

meditation

Skills practised

- Literacy: considering different meanings of key Sikh phrases
- Thinking: unpicking the concept of spiritual darkness and light
- Evaluation: examining key Sikh beliefs about God and creation
- Reflection: reflecting on what they believe about the existence and nature of God

Resources

- 1.2 Beliefs Worksheet: students complete a flow chart on Sikh beliefs about God
- 1.2 Waheguru Interactive Activity: students sort statements about Waheguru according to whether Sikhs do or do not believe in them
- 1.2 Lesson Player: a ready-to-go presentation with built-in resources and teacher notes
- 1 Image Gallery: a useful gallery of photos and film stills from the chapter
- 1.2 Self-Assessment Sheet: students evaluate their learning against the lesson objectives

Ideas for starters

1. Use the Starter from the *Student Book*.
2. Ask the class if they know any (inoffensive!) 'chants'. For example, from rugby or football, or songs they know. Ask what their purpose might be.
3. Hand out mini-whiteboards if you have them, or plain paper with coloured pens, and get students to write down as many words as they can which are special to them, even if they are

just the names of their family and/or friends. They should then explain to a partner, or share with the class, why they chose those words.

4. Ask students to write down three things they know about Sikhs – one they are sure of and two they think are true.

Activity guidance

- When students are considering light and dark, you could use a candle or lamp and darken the surrounding room to aid their reflections.
- You may wish to compare God in Sikhism with other faiths. See Unit 1.2 in the *Islam Student Book*, Unit 1.1 in the *Christianity Student Book*, and Units 1.1–1.2 in the *Hinduism Student Book*.

Ideas for plenaries

1. Use the Reflection from the *Student Book*.
2. Take the class outside and ask them to look around at what they see in the natural world, or show them images of local areas. Ask whether they can see any evidence of a creative force, or whether they see something different. Encourage them to reflect on their observations by feeding back to each other in pairs, to the class, or in their books.
3. Encourage peer assessment in the symbol/collage activity in the *Student Book*, by using 'two stars and a wish' – two things that were good and one thing to work on for next time.

Further class and homework activities

1. Use students' work on Activity 4 in the *Student Book* to compile a list of questions that they wanted to ask about the Sikh view of God. Then, as a class, choose one and try to answer it. Once you have done this in class, set students the task of asking this question at home, or of their friends/family, and writing up the results.
2. Ask students to list key words that describe God from other faiths they are studying and identify any similarities or differences.
3. You could start the lesson with a stilling exercise. These can be found on the Internet and should not have a religious theme, but focus more on relaxation. This will encourage students to think about a meditative approach.
4. As a homework activity, ask students to research how the symbolism of light overcoming darkness is used in other faiths, e.g. Christianity and Hinduism.
5. 1.2 Beliefs Worksheet on the *Sikhism OxBox Online*.
6. 1.2 Waheguru Interactive Activity on the *Sikhism OxBox Online*.
7. Further suggestions on page 24 of this book.

1.3 Soldiers and Saints: The Symbolism of the Khanda

The unit in brief

The unit looks at the Sikh emblem (the Khanda) and the Reht Maryada (the Sikh code of conduct). A case study family explains why the Khanda is significant for Sikhs.

Key ideas

- The Khanda has symbolic significance and is the Sikh emblem
- The Reht Maryada is the Sikh code of conduct
- Sikhs have to complete three main duties in life: praying, working honestly, and giving

Skills practised

- Application: applying key symbols and beliefs to the practices of a Sikh family
- Thinking: considering how religious symbols may impact on a person's life
- Literacy: analysing the three main duties from the Rahit Maryada
- Reflection: reflecting on whether or not duties should be performed for a reward

Resources

- 1.3 Khanda Film Clip: Tohmev and Mr Singh explain what different parts of the Khanda symbol represent
- 1.3 Film Worksheet: students assess their understanding of the case study film clip by linking ideas to the *Student Book*
- 1.3 Code of Conduct Interactive Activity: students fill the gaps in a paragraph about the Sikh code of conduct
- 1.3 Lesson Player: a ready to go presentation with built in resources and teacher notes
- 1 Image Gallery: a useful gallery of photos and film stills from the chapter
- 1.3 Self-Assessment Sheet: students evaluate their learning against the lesson objectives

Ideas for starters

1. Use the Starter from the *Student Book*.
2. Put an image of the Khanda on the board (see 1 Image Gallery on the *Sikhism OxBox Online*) and ask students what they think the different elements might mean.
3. Ask students – from what they know about Sikhism so far – what the Sikh 'code of conduct' might contain. How would key beliefs be put into action?

Activity guidance

- Activity 4 in the *Student Book*, which asks students to design their own logo, could be a time-management task, e.g. students have only five minutes. It could then be followed up or completed as homework.
- Spend time as a class discussing the three main duties and the activity linked to them. These are fundamental parts of the Sikh faith and daily life.

Ideas for plenaries

1. Use the Reflection from the *Student Book*.
2. Ask students to create a quiz of five to ten questions for a partner to answer. As an extension, the partners not only have to give answers, but also explain what the answers mean.
3. Ask students to suggest ways in which duties might benefit or detract from daily life, and give reasons.
4. Ask students to consider what they have learned about Sikh beliefs on God over the past two units. Then ask them to create a mind-map to show the different aspects they have studied.

Further class and homework activities

1. Use 1.3 Code of Conduct Interactive Activity on the *Sikhism OxBox Online* to consolidate students' learning about the meaning and purpose of the Khanda/Reht Maryada.
2. Show 1.3 Khanda Film Clip on the *Sikhism OxBox Online*.
3. 1.3 Film Worksheet on the *Sikhism OxBox Online*.
4. Further suggestions on page 24 of this book.

1.4 After Death, After Life – What Lives On?

The unit in brief

This unit looks at the Sikh beliefs about life after death and, through a case study, the different actions and choices that a Sikh can make to influence and affect this life and the next.

Key ideas

- Sikhs believe in life after death, and reincarnation
- The ultimate goal is to gain mukti for the soul, which is union with God
- The actions of a person have an impact on this life, and their afterlife

Useful Words

gurmukh, karma, manmukh, mukti, reincarnation, soul (atma)

Skills practised

- Thinking: considering how beliefs may impact both this life and the next
- Reflection: considering ways in which life can be lived as 'manmukh' or 'gurmukh'
- Literacy: interpreting the key words and ideas in teachings and beliefs
- Interpretation: linking interpretations of the afterlife together

Resources

- 1.4 Chitar and Gupat Film Clip: Balwir Singh tells the story of how actions in our life are recorded by the angels, Chitar and Gupat
- 1.4 Film Worksheet: students assess their understanding of the case study film clip by linking ideas to the *Student Book*
- 1.4 Life After Death Interactive Activity: students link key terms to their definitions
- 1.4 Lesson Player: a ready-to-go presentation with built-in resources and teacher notes
- 1 Image Gallery: a useful gallery of photos and film stills from the chapter
- 1.4 Self-Assessment Sheet: students evaluate their learning against the lesson objectives

Ideas for starters

1. Use the Starter from the *Student Book*. Ask them what they think of the idea that human beings might have a 'soul' or a 'spirit'.
2. Ask students to create a sentence explaining what they believe about life after death, even if it is 'I don't know'. Discuss as a class, encouraging students to show awareness of what factors have influenced their thoughts.

3. Put up an atmospheric image of the sky with clouds and ask why some people see this as an image of the afterlife. This could lead into the contrasting idea of reincarnation.
4. Ask students to name five things that humans do in this life that have clear consequences. Is it possible that actions might have consequences in an afterlife?

Activity guidance

- Starter activity 2 could be used to fill the board full of key ideas and terms that might, in turn, create questions that could stimulate some great discussions. Don't be afraid to go off course for a while.
- Activity 1 in the *Student Book* requires students to prepare something for a Year 5 class. It might be worth identifying the basic level of understanding that a Year 5 student has.
- You may wish to compare Sikh teachings about the afterlife with those of other faiths. See Units 2.5–2.6 in the *Christianity Student Book*.

Ideas for plenaries

1. Use the Reflection from the *Student Book*.
2. Stage a class debate about whether there is an afterlife. Students should try to refer to Sikh teachings when explaining their views.
3. Ask students to take a look at the five Sikh vices mentioned by Balwir Singh (lust, greed, attachment to things of this world, anger, and pride) and compare them with the three main duties from the previous unit. Discuss whether or not one helps to contain the other.

Further class and homework activities

1. Ask students: if everyone believed there was a divine spark in all humans, what difference might this make to everyday life?
2. As a homework activity, ask students whether they think the Sikh view is a fair way of seeing life and death. Ask them to compare the Sikh position with the views of a faith that doesn't believe in reincarnation. Would this version be fairer?
3. Use 1.4 Life After Death Interactive Activity on the *Sikhism OxBox Online* to consolidate students' learning about key beliefs and definitions in Sikhism.
4. Show 1.4 Chitar and Gupat Film Clip on the *Sikhism OxBox Online*.
5. 1.4 Film Worksheet on the *Sikhism OxBox Online*.
6. Further suggestions on page 24 of this book.

Chapter 1 Further Suggestions

These suggestions are addressed directly to students.

1.1 What is at the Root of Sikhism?

1 If you were to put one person at the centre of your life – famous or not, alive or dead – who would it be and why? Think carefully about how you explain your choice, because this is an important skill. *

2 Design a five- or six-word greeting to use with your friends that represents who you are and what you stand for. *

3 If Guru Nanak came into your lesson to introduce the Mool Mantar and explain why it's so significant, what do you think he would say? **

4 Create a word cloud that is all about the Mool Mantar, but doesn't include any of the key words from it. Think about what the key words mean and choose ones that mean the same to go into the word cloud. **

1.2 Who is Waheguru?

1 Using the information in this unit, create a sentence that sums up how Sikhs might describe God. *

2 In groups, explain what your responses are to Sikh beliefs about God in nature. Are your responses similar or different in any way? **

3 Complete a class survey about beliefs in God – asking questions about what people believe God is like (all powerful, creator, etc.). Create a graphical representation of the results and then compare them with what Sikhism says God is like. **

4 Do you think that most people in this world are theists (people who believe in God), atheists (people who do not believe in God) or agnostics (people who do not know what they believe about God)? Why? ***

5 What do you think are the strengths and weaknesses of what Sikhism teaches about God? ***

6 If you could create your own God, what would they be like and why? Pay attention to how you explain/justify your choices, because this is a useful skill. **

7 If, tomorrow, everyone were to start believing in God – as described by Sikhism – would the world change? **

1.3 Soldiers and Saints: The Symbolism of the Khanda

1 Pray, work honestly, and give are the three main duties laid out in the Reht Maryada. Choose one of the three and create a flier that explains why it should apply to everyone, from the Sikh point of view. **

2 If you were to create a wordsearch or crossword to go with this unit, which ten words would you choose? *

3 Research what two other faiths say about duty and compare them with Sikhism. ***

4 Write a three-day blog for someone following the Reht Maryada for the first time. What would be the easiest/hardest things to do? **

1.4 After Death, After Life – What Lives On?

1 Take the following words, manmukh, gurmukh, karma and reincarnation, and use them to create a role-play on Sikh beliefs about life after death. **

2 Do you think there will come a time when everyone believes in life after death? Give your reasons. **

3 Create a forum or discussion board for a website that has two people arguing about life after death. What two different things could they be arguing for or against, and what would they say? **

4 'We should all be allowed a second chance.' Do you agree? Is reincarnation the same thing as a second (third, fourth ...) chance? ***

5 Would you live your life differently if you believed that everything you did had either a good or bad consequence at some point? Explain your answer. **

Chapter 1 Assessment

Assessment in the *Student Book*

You will find an assessment task at the end of every chapter which focuses on AT2. In this chapter, the task asks students to prepare a presentation or a leaflet to be used as a resource in RE, in answer to the question: Who is a Sikh?

In the *Student Book* (and on the supporting worksheets), you'll find guidance about levels of assessment that you can use to help your students understand what their work should include. You could ask them to use these criteria for self- or peer-assessment once they've completed the task.

> **Living Faiths Assessment**
>
> ***Student Book***
> - Assessment Task
> - Levels Guidance
>
> ***OxBox Online***
> - Auto-Marked Test
> - Assessment Task Presentation
> - Assessment Worksheets

Assessment Task for Chapter 1 (pages **16–17** of the *Sikhism Student Book*)

Objectives

- Explore and apply the key beliefs that Sikhs have about God and duty.
- Reflect on your own ideas about God and the responsibilities you have in your life.

Task

Prepare a presentation or a leaflet to be used as a resource in RE, in answer to the question: Who is a Sikh? You will need to explain what Sikhs believe about God, including the significance of the Mool Mantar. The final part of your presentation or leaflet should contain your own reflections about core Sikh beliefs.

Assessment in *OxBox Online*

On the *Sikhism OxBox Online*, you'll find resources to use when introducing the assessment task to the class.

You can use the *Chapter 1 Assessment Task Presentation* as a front-of-class tool to help your students unpack the assessment criteria, and understand what is expected of them.

Chapter 1 Assessment Worksheets accompany the task, so that once you finish the presentation, your students can easily get started.

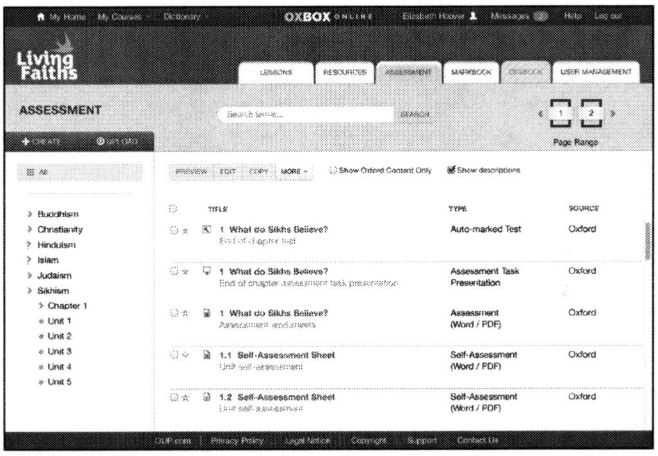

▲ Assessment resources for Chapter 1 on the *Sikhism Oxbox Online*

Auto-marked tests

The *Sikhism OxBox Online* also contains auto-marked tests for each chapter to help save you time setting questions and marking for AT1. The test for this chapter contains 15 questions and will take most students about half an hour. Test results are automatically stored in the markbook.

Digital markbook

A markbook and a reporting function complete the *OxBox Online* assessment package, so you can keep all your students' test results and assessment scores in one place. This can include the auto-marked tests as well as pieces of work you or the students have marked by hand.

Chapter 2 Overview
Where do Sikh Beliefs Come From?

Helping you deliver Key Stage 3 RE

This chapter addresses the following areas of the Programme of Study:

Key concepts

Beliefs, teachings and sources

- Interpreting teachings, sources, authorities (including the Guru Granth Sahib and the ten Sikh Gurus) and ways of life in order to understand religions and beliefs

Practices and ways of life

- Understanding that religious practices are diverse, change over time and are influenced by cultures

Key processes

Learning about religion

- Investigate the impact of religious beliefs and teachings on individuals, communities and societies, the reasons for commitment and the causes of diversity
- Explain religious beliefs, practices and commitments, including their transmission by people, texts and traditions
- Interpret a range of sources, texts, authorities, and forms of religious and spiritual expression from a variety of contexts

Learning from religion

- Reflect on the relationship between beliefs, teachings, world issues and ultimate questions
- Express their own beliefs and ideas, using a variety of forms of expression, including creative forms and reasoned arguments

The big picture

These are the key ideas behind this chapter:

- Guru Nanak founded Sikhism after undergoing a religious experience.
- The word Guru means teacher. Sikhism had ten human Gurus, who all added something to the evolution of the faith.
- The Guru Granth Sahib is the Sikh holy book, which contains the teachings of the ten human Gurus (as well as elements from Hindu and Muslim saints).
- The Khalsa is the community of initiated Sikhs started in 1699 by Guru Gobind Singh.

Chapter outline

Use this to give students a mental road map of the chapter:

2.1 Guru Nanak Sahib Ji – explains the role of Guru Nanak in founding Sikhism

2.2 What Makes a Great Teacher? – considers the role of Guru Nanak as a teacher

2.3 The Tremendous Ten (Part A) – introduces the first five Sikh Gurus

2.4 The Tremendous Ten (Part B) – introduces the remaining five Sikh Gurus

2.5 Why is the Eternal Guru Special? – examines the importance of the Guru Granth Sahib (the Sikh holy book)

2.6 The Faithful Followers: The Revelation of the Khalsa – explains how the Khalsa was revealed

Opportunities for assessment

Summative assessments on the *Sikhism OxBox Online* include automarked tests, interactive activities, and self-assessment worksheets.

The end-of-chapter assessment task in the *Student Book* provides formative assessment. Supporting materials for the assessment task can be found on the *Sikhism OxBox Online*, such as the Assessment Task Presentation and the related worksheets.

There are other opportunities for assessment too. For example, you could use some of the activities or reflection points throughout each *Student Book* unit, or some of the 'Further Suggestions' at the end of this chapter.

Getting ready for this chapter

- Students will probably have completed work on units that look at some key teachings and themes in Sikhism, which will help them in their understanding. If they haven't done as yet, it could be beneficial to spend a little time exploring some of the basics from the first chapter.
- If you have the *Sikhism OxBox Online*, watch the case study film clips in advance, so that you can prepare and guide students before and during their viewing.

Objectives and outcomes for this chapter

Objectives	Unit	Outcomes
Most students will:		Most students will be able to:
• explain the relevance of Guru Nanak's upbringing and teaching • analyse the nature of a religious experience • reflect on their own life-changing experiences.	**2.1**	• describe Guru Nanak's early life • discuss the idea of a religious experience, with reference to Guru Nanak's experience • consider their own life-changing experiences and how they were affected.
• identify some of Guru Nanak's key teachings • explain the role of Guru Nanak's teachings in a Sikh's life • reflect on the qualities of a good teacher.	**2.2**	• describe some of Guru Nanak's key teachings, and the story of Malik Bhago and Bhai Lalo • explain the importance of Guru Nanak to all Sikhs today • consider what makes a good teacher and how this impacts their learning.
• explain the role and significance of the ten Sikh Gurus • explain the impacts of the lives and actions of the Gurus • explore to what extent a role model can 'lead'.	**2.3**	• describe something of the life of each of the ten human Gurus • describe what each of the ten human Gurus added to the development of Sikhism through their teachings and actions.
• explain the role and significance of the ten Sikh Gurus • explain the impacts of the lives and actions of the Gurus • explore to what extent a role model can 'lead'.	**2.4**	• describe something of the life of each of the ten human Gurus • describe what each of the ten human Gurus added to the development of Sikhism through their teachings and actions.
• identify the relationship between the ten human Gurus and the Guru Granth Sahib • examine the significance of the Guru Granth Sahib for Sikhs • reflect on the topic of respect.	**2.5**	• describe the part played by the ten human Gurus in the development of the content of the Guru Granth Sahib • explain that the Guru Granth Sahib is the Eternal Guru, and that it provides answers for Sikhs to any questions they might have in their lives.
• explain the origins of the Khalsa • interpret the meaning of faith • reflect on personal commitment and what it involves.	**2.6**	• describe the story of the Khalsa, and explore the deeper meanings by generating philosophical questions • consider the role played by faith in the formation of the Panj Piare • reflect on what makes them put their trust in someone.

2.1 Guru Nanak Sahib Ji

The unit in brief

This unit explores the early life of Guru Nanak, and how events led him to become the founder of Sikhism. It also explores the value of religious experiences.

Key ideas

- Guru Nanak is the founder of Sikhism
- He received enlightenment about the importance of worshipping one God
- He had a life-changing, religious experience at the age of 30

Useful Words

religious experience, sacred thread

Skills practised

- Enquiry: exploring the story of Guru Nanak's religious experience through philosophical questioning
- Thinking: considering the ways in which beliefs can be expressed through art
- Evaluation: evaluating the idea of having a direct experience of God
- Reflection: reflecting on whether students have ever had a life-changing experience

Resources

- 2.1 Guru Nanak Audio Clip: the story of Guru Nanak and the river from the *Student Book*
- 2.1 Key Teachings Worksheet: students complete a mind map about the teachings of Guru Nanak
- 2.1 Guru Nanak Interactive Activity: students decide what Guru Nanak learned from his enlightenment from a list of options
- 2.1 Lesson Player: a ready-to-go presentation with built-in resources and teacher notes
- 2 Image Gallery: a useful gallery of photos and film stills from the chapter
- 2.1 Self-Assessment Sheet: students evaluate their learning against the lesson objectives

Ideas for starters

1. Use the Starter from the *Student Book*.
2. Ask students to describe the leadership or inspirational qualities of a famous person, with the rest of the class trying to guess who they are.
3. Ask students what they think is meant by the phrase 'religious experience'. Have they ever heard of any examples? Would they ever want to have one? Why or why not? Discussions could take place in groups.
4. Ask students what characteristics they would like to have that they admire in others.

Activity guidance

- The activity in the *Student Book* text about the picture of Guru Nanak works very well with a little preparation. Remind students that cameras didn't exist at this time, and artists often used interpretation and symbolism in their work. Ask what they think the artist was trying to emphasize.
- The activity in the *Student Book* directly related to the story of Guru Nanak and the river asks if it's possible to experience a divine being. Students who do not believe in God can be encouraged to express this and discuss how it makes them feel to read about religious experiences.
- Activity 1 in the *Student Book* is a good opportunity for a Community of Enquiry, in which students generate philosophical questions in groups, and then vote on what they want to discuss further.

Ideas for plenaries

1. Use the Reflection from the *Student Book*.
2. Ask students to imagine that they were with Guru Nanak, moments after coming out of the river, when he was enlightened. What questions would they ask him? Could they imagine what answers he might give?
3. Take a class vote to find out how many students think that some kind of religious experience is possible. Have a 'hands down' policy and ask individual students to justify their choices.
4. Hold a small group or class debate about the statement: 'Religious experiences prove the existence of a God.'
5. Ask students to focus on the quotation from the Guru Granth Sahib in the *Student Book*. To what extent do they think followers of different faiths would agree? What might be the arguments against this?

Further class and homework activities

1. Ask students to research a little more about Guru Nanak's enlightenment, and then design a multiple-choice quiz based on what they find out.
2. Ask students to create their 'ultimate leader'. Would they be male/female/have no gender? What would their characteristics be? What actions would they take? Would they have had an experience of some kind, in the way that Guru Nanak did?
3. What qualities would a person need to have in order to change their religion, and what difficulties might they have to overcome?
4. As homework, ask students to research Buddha's enlightenment and compare the two enlightenment stories.
5. 2.1 Guru Nanak Audio Clip on the *Sikhism OxBox Online*.
6. 2.1 Key Teachings Worksheet on the *Sikhism OxBox Online*.
7. 2.1 Guru Nanak Interactive Activity on the *Sikhism OxBox Online*.
8. Further suggestions on page 40 of this book.

2.2 What Makes a Great Teacher?

The unit in brief

This unit looks at Guru Nanak as a teacher, and some of the stories that he told. It also looks at the importance of Guru Nanak in the lives of individual Sikhs, with the help of a case study.

Key ideas

- Guru Nanak was a wise and holy teacher
- His key stories and teachings can be found in the Guru Granth Sahib
- Key teachings include contemplating on God, and sharing with others.

Skills practised

- Analysis: analysing the story of Malik Bhago and Bhai Lalo
- Application: applying the themes and principles found in the teachings to their own lives and the lives of others
- Enquiry: asking questions of the case study speaker about the three duties
- Reflection: reflecting on how and when they learn best

Resources

- 2.2 Malik Bhago Audio Clip: the story of Malik Bhago and Bhai Lalo from the *Student Book*
- 2.2 Guru Nanak Film Clip: Tohmev, Mrs Kaur and Mr Singh explain the role that Guru Nanak plays in their lives
- 2.2 Film Worksheet: students assess their understanding of the case study film clip by linking ideas to the *Student Book*
- 2.2 Bhago and Lalo Interactive Activity: students decide whether statements about the story of Malik Bhago and Bhai Lalo are true or false
- 2.2 Lesson Player: a ready-to-go presentation with built-in resources and teacher notes
- 2 Image Gallery: a useful gallery of photos and film stills from the chapter
- 2.2 Self-Assessment Sheet: students evaluate their learning against the lesson objectives

Ideas for starters

1. Use the Starter from the *Student Book*.
2. Ask students to think about the possible themes that they would expect a religious teacher to talk about. They should begin on their own and then 'snowball' out into pairs, fours and so on.
3. Get students to come up with one phrase or saying that they think is really good and should be shared with others. Begin sharing, ensuring that a full explanation is given.

4. 'Without one person leading the way, nothing can ever happen.' Ask whether students agree with this statement or not. Then ask for some reasons why or why not.

Activity guidance

- The Starter in the *Student Book* is about the environment in which students learn best, so encourage them to spend time thinking about what works for them.
- The full story of Malik Bhago and Bhai Lalo could provide the basis of deeper reflection as part of a Community of Enquiry.
- You could compare the teachings of Guru Nanak with Jesus. See Unit 1.3 in the *Christianity Student Book*.

Ideas for plenaries

1. Use the Reflection from the *Student Book*.
2. Ask students to role-play, as if they were Sikhs, discussing how and why the teachings of Guru Nanak are so valued.
3. **a)** Ask students to imagine that Guru Nanak is about to set up a school nearby. Their job is to design an emblem for that school to reflect the kind of leader/teacher that Nanak was.
   b) Draw up an advertisement for the post of Head teacher at the school. What qualities would be required?
   c) What would be on the school curriculum? What might the school have that other schools would not have?

Further class and homework activities

1. As homework, ask students to apply their learning and create a short story that they think might be similar to those of Guru Nanak.
2. Use 2.2 Bhago and Lalo Interactive Activity on the *Sikhism OxBox Online* to consolidate students' learning about some of the key teachings.
3. 2.2 Guru Nanak Film Clip on the *Sikhism OxBox Online*.
4. 2.2 Film Worksheet on the *Sikhism OxBox Online*.
5. 2.2 Malik Bhago Audio Clip on the *Sikhism OxBox Online*.
6. Further suggestions on page 40 of this book.

2.3 The Tremendous Ten (Part A)

The unit in brief

This unit and the next (2.4) explore the lives of the ten Sikh Gurus – highlighting key historical events, actions and choices that the Gurus made.

Key ideas

- The first five Sikh Gurus were called Guru Nanak, Guru Angad, Guru Amar Das, Guru Ram Das and Guru Arjan
- Even though the teachings of all the Gurus were the same, each Guru is known for something different about the Sikh faith

Useful Words

castes, creeds, pilgrimage

Skills practised

- Thinking: considering what tests Guru Nanak may have put his successor through
- Reflection: reflecting on the concepts of class and equality in modern-day society
- Empathy: discussing the possible reasons behind religious intolerance

Resources

- 2.3 Guru Arjan Worksheet: students conduct further research into Guru Arjan and answer questions
- 2.3 Gurus Interactive Activity: students link Gurus with their contributions to Sikhism
- 2.3 Lesson Player: a ready-to-go presentation with built-in resources and teacher notes
- 2 Image Gallery: a useful gallery of photos and film stills from the chapter
- 2.3 Self-Assessment Sheet: students evaluate their learning against the lesson objectives

Ideas for starters

1. Use the Starter from the *Student Book*.
2. Put up images of people, places or words that inspire you (as a teacher) and ask students to suggest reasons why they might be inspirational.
3. Ask students to imagine that they are the king or queen. Ask them what sort of people they would want around them at all times to guide and protect them.

Activity guidance

- In order to demonstrate how the Starter in the *Student Book* works, you could suggest the superhero you would most like to be and why.
- You could adapt the activity in the *Student Book* about Guru Nanak testing Guru Angad by turning it into an X factor-style task. What does Guru Angad need to achieve to get through to the next round?
- To help students with the Reflection in the *Student Book*, you may need to explain what a Haiku is (a poem of seventeen syllables, in three lines of five, seven, and five).

Ideas for plenaries

1. Use the Reflection from the *Student Book*.
2. Ask students who they turn to for advice on things that really matter.
3. Ask students to create a spoken verse or rap that will help them to remember some or all of the first five Gurus and their contributions.
4. Ask students to choose which of the first five Gurus is the one they would like to be like most, or the one they admire most. Ask for their reasons.

Further class and homework activities

1. Ask students to produce a two-part documentary about the impact of the Gurus (focusing, in particular, on two Gurus of their choice). They have to look only at the impact they had – this is not a biography of their lives. The first part of the documentary should be based on one of the Gurus from Unit 2.3, and the second part on one of the Gurus from Unit 2.4.
2. As homework, ask students to design a building that they would be happy to leave behind as their legacy (as both Guru Ram Das and Guru Arjan did). What would need to be in it? How would it highlight what was important to them?
3. At either the end of Unit 2.3, or after Unit 2.4 has been completed as well, ask students to create a multiple-choice quiz with at least ten questions. The focus must be on the contributions of the Gurus and not a fact-file/biography.
4. 2.3 Guru Arjan Worksheet on the *Sikhism OxBox Online*.
5. 2.3 Gurus Interactive Activity on the *Sikhism OxBox Online*.
6. Further suggestions on page 40 of this book.

2.4 The Tremendous Ten (Part B)

The unit in brief

This is the second unit on the ten Sikh Gurus. It explores the lives and contributions of the remaining five Gurus and highlights key historical events, actions and choices that these Gurus made.

Key ideas

- The final five Sikh Gurus were called Guru Har Gobind, Guru Har Rai, Guru Har Krishan, Guru Tegh Bahadur and Guru Gobind Singh
- even though the teachings of all the Gurus were the same, each Guru is known for something different about the Sikh faith

Skills practised

- Literacy: writing a magazine interview with two of the Gurus; creating an advertisement; writing a letter to a teenage head teacher
- Thinking: considering the relative importance of earthly and spiritual authority
- Reflection: reflecting on the role of leadership

Resources

- 2.4 Gurus Worksheet: small groups of students produce a speech advocating a particular Guru, with a final class vote deciding which Guru wins
- 2.4 Gurus Interactive Activity: students link Gurus with their contributions to Sikhism
- 2.4 Lesson Player: a ready-to-go presentation with built-in resources and teacher notes
- 2 Image Gallery: a useful gallery of photos and film stills from the chapter
- 2.4 Self-Assessment Sheet: students evaluate their learning against the lesson objectives

Ideas for starters

1. To remind students about the five Gurus they have already studied in Unit 2.3, get them to do a Reduced Shakespeare-style performance to recap the topic so far.
2. Ask the class what they think the remaining five human Gurus might have contributed to Sikhism, knowing what they already know about the first five.
3. Ask students to create a list of the ten people they would have as Gurus in their own lives, with reasons.

Activity guidance

You may wish to talk through the activity in the *Student Book* on children in positions of authority. Students may find it difficult to imagine at first, but it will be challenging and worthwhile!

Ideas for plenaries

1. Use the Reflection from the *Student Book*.
2. Ask students if they could invite one of the ten human Gurus to come and speak at a school assembly, who it would be and why.
3. Get a selection of students to come up, and – for each of the ten Gurus – summarize the impact they think the Gurus had on the development of Sikhism.
4. Repeat plenaries 2 or 3 from Unit 2.3 for the remaining five Gurus.

Further class and homework activities

1. Ask students to prepare part two of their documentary on the impact of the Gurus (see Activity 1 in Further class and homework activities for Unit 2.3), based on the five Gurus discussed in Unit 2.4.
2. Use 2.4 Gurus Worksheet on the *Sikhism OxBox Online* to prepare for and complete a class vote about the most popular or influential Guru.
3. Use 2.4 Gurus Interactive Activity on the *Sikhism OxBox Online* to focus students on some of the main themes found in the Gurus' teachings.
4. Further suggestions on page 40 of this book.

2.5 Why is the Eternal Guru Special?

The unit in brief

This unit uses case study material to help examine the Guru Granth Sahib – its origins, what it contains, why it's important to Sikhs, and how Sikhs show respect for it.

Key ideas

- The Guru Granth Sahib is the Sikh holy book
- It is treated with great respect by Sikhs
- It is made up of the teachings and writings of the ten Sikh Gurus
- It also contains holy writings from Hindu and Muslim saints

Skills practised

- Thinking: considering why the Guru Granth Sahib is significant and how it plays a role in the life of a Sikh
- Evaluation: evaluating the benefits for a Sikh in reading the Guru Granth Sahib regularly
- Reflection: reflecting on whether there is enough respect in the world today

Resources

- 2.5 Guru Granth Sahib Film Clip: Balwir Singh explains why the Guru Granth Sahib is important to Sikhs
- 2.5 Film Worksheet: students assess their understanding of the case study film clip by linking ideas to the *Student Book*
- 2.5 Guru Granth Sahib Interactive Activity: students select true statements about the Guru Granth Sahib
- 2.5 Lesson Player: a ready-to-go presentation with built-in resources and teacher notes
- 2 Image Gallery: a useful gallery of photos and film stills from the chapter
- 2.5 Self-Assessment Sheet: students evaluate their learning against the lesson objectives

Ideas for starters

1. Use the Starter from the *Student Book*.
2. Ask students how they treat something that is precious to them.
3. Hold up two or three of your favourite books and describe why they are significant to you. Explain how you treat them, who you share them with, and so on. Encourage students to explain the significance of their own favourite books.

4. An extension of the above might be to have 'circle time' and read a segment of your favourite book – you could prep the students by asking them to bring in segments too, ready for the lesson. Share as a class the words that are special to you.

Activity guidance

Balwir Singh is very passionate about his faith and reading the Guru Granth Sahib. He talks about the Guru Granth Sahib being available online. If possible, take students to the ICT room and get them to look it up. Ask them to describe what they think Balwir's experience of the Guru Granth Sahib is online.
How would it compare to having it in front of him?

Ideas for plenaries

1. Use the Reflection from the *Student Book*.
2. Get the class to stand up, and then ask them questions about the material in this unit, which involve 'yes' or 'no' answers. Explain that they have to stand up for yes and sit for no. You can check their understanding and reinforce learning in this way.
3. Ask students to look at the unit's Learning Objectives and reflect on how well they think they have met them. Ask them to explain how they met them and what skills they think they have practised.

Further class and homework activities

1. As homework, ask students to do some research to find out how holy books are treated in other faiths.
2. As another homework, ask students to create a guide for a young Sikh on how to use the Guru Granth Sahib. They may have to do a little extra research.
3. Use 2.5 Guru Granth Sahib Interactive Activity on the *Sikhism OxBox Online* to consolidate students' learning about some of the key elements of the Guru Granth Sahib.
4. 2.5 Guru Granth Sahib Film Clip on the *Sikhism OxBox Online*.
5. 2.5 Film Worksheet on the *Sikhism OxBox Online*.
6. Further suggestions on page 40 of this book.

2.6 The Faithful Followers: The Revelation of the Khalsa

The unit in brief

This unit explores the origin of the Khalsa, and the part that Guru Gobind Singh played in it. It also aims to allow students the chance to explore their own ideas about faith and sacrifice.

Key ideas

- The Khalsa originated in 1699 at the celebration of Vaisakhi
- It was instituted by Guru Gobind Singh, who tested his followers' faith
- The Khalsa is the community of Sikhs who have decided to show further commitment to their faith
- Sikhs undertake the Amrit ceremony to join the Khalsa, which is open to everyone

Skills practised

- Application: exploring the ways that faith can play a role in people's lives
- Thinking skills: considering the responses people may have to situations involving sacrifice
- Literacy: creating written responses to the story in this unit
- Reflection: considering what makes them put their trust in someone

Resources

- 2.6 Panj Piare Audio Clip: the story of the Khalsa from the *Student Book*
- 2.6 Khalsa Worksheet: students sort key words from the text into an appropriate order, before using them to discuss the Khalsa with a partner
- 2.6 Khalsa Interactive Activity: students drag events from the story of the revelation of the Khalsa into the correct order
- 2.6 Lesson Player: a ready-to-go presentation with built-in resources and teacher notes
- 2 Image Gallery: a useful gallery of photos and film stills from the chapter
- 2.6 Self-Assessment Sheet: students evaluate their learning against the lesson objectives

Ideas for starters

1. Use the Starter from the *Student Book*.
2. Ask students to list on a mini-whiteboard or sheet of paper the people, objects, or ideas they would be happy to sacrifice something for.

3. Ask students to consider – if they had created their own secret or special society – what rituals or processes people would have to perform in order to join it.
4. Ask students whether they think it's acceptable to test people in order to win or prove their loyalty.
5. It's said that faith can move mountains, figuratively speaking. Ask students why they think faith is so powerful. Do they think it's more powerful than physical strength? Why or why not?
6. Ask students what they think inspires faith. Is faith the same as trust?

Activity guidance

- There are a number of specific terms or phrases used in this unit. Get the students to familiarize themselves with them before you read through the unit and/or do the activities.
- Activity 2 in the *Student Book* is a good opportunity for a Community of Enquiry. In groups, students should generate interesting, philosophical questions, and then vote on which question they would like to discuss and present to the rest of the class. The class can then respond with more questions.

Ideas for plenaries

1. Use the Reflection from the *Student Book*.
2. Ask students, individually or in pairs, to create an emblem that could be worn as a badge, showing that the wearer has faith in faith. Then they should create a second emblem that they think a Sikh might wear.
3. Ask students to reflect on who they think their 'Panj Piare' would be.
4. Ask students how the Khalsa demonstrates equality.

Further class and homework activities

1. As homework, ask students to create an animation or documentary that follows either Guru Gobind Singh on the day he established the Khalsa, or a Sikh joining the Khalsa and receiving Amrit.
2. As another homework, ask students to plan and prepare a 30-second TV advert that encourages the watcher to have faith in something. It could be faith in themselves, another person, or a deity.
3. 2.6 Panj Piare Audio Clip on the *Sikhism OxBox Online*.
4. 2.6 Khalsa Worksheet on the *Sikhism OxBox Online*.
5. 2.6 Khalsa Interactive Activity on the *Sikhism OxBox Online*.
6. Further suggestions on page 40 of this book.

Chapter 2 Further Suggestions

These suggestions are addressed directly to students.

2.1 Guru Nanak Sahib Ji

1. Research the life of Guru Nanak after his enlightenment. Where did he go? Who did he see? What do you think these experiences would have given Guru Nanak in his work? *
2. Design an object or symbol that you think would represent the life of Guru Nanak – without drawing him. *
3. Think about the themes found in Guru Nanak's life and teachings. In groups, create role plays that demonstrate these themes for the modern world in a modern context. **
4. Why do you think there were so many difficulties between Hindus and Muslims at the time? Do some research and write a paragraph to explain your findings. ***

2.2 What Makes a Great Teacher?

1. Look up further examples of the teachings of Guru Nanak and pick out ten Key words from them. Then create a visual piece to explain Guru Nanak's teachings, using your ten words. **
2. Create a set of ten questions that you would like to ask Guru Nanak. Explain why you have chosen them. *
3. Prepare and present a role play that has Guru Nanak appearing on a chat show. What questions would you ask and how do you think he would answer? **
4. Suggest ways in which Guru Nanak's teachings could be represented purely as visual pieces with no words. *
5. Explore how the teachings of Guru Nanak compare with the teachings of Jesus. Can you see any common themes? Are these themes central to humanity? ***

2.3 The Tremendous Ten (Part A)

1. Create a flow chart for the first five Gurus, giving each one a new piece of information explaining what they contributed to Sikhism. *
2. Create a list of who's who in your life – explaining why each person is significant to you. *
3. Many of the Gurus fought for the freedom of others to express their beliefs or religion. Create a leaflet or manifesto that explains what you would be prepared to fight for. ***
4. Write the script for a radio show on which three of the Gurus are guests. Choose which Gurus you want to include and decide what you think they would say. **

2.4 The Tremendous Ten (Part B)

1. Create a 15-question quiz about the ten Gurus, with at least five symbol or image questions. Quiz your classmates to see who can get the highest score. *
2. Imagine that you are designing a festival that all ten Gurus will attend. You have to set up a tent for each of them. Choose five Gurus and create the tent design, explaining what will happen in each and why. **
3. Assess the value of having a range of people who have contributed to the teachings of a faith (as opposed to just one or two). ***
4. Prepare information about one of the Gurus for a hot-seat task. By only asking 'yes or no' questions, the rest of the class have to guess who you have chosen. *
5. Create a whole-class mural that, using no words, explores what the Gurus contributed to the development of Sikhism. **

2.5 Why is the Eternal Guru Special?

1. Create a social network profile for the Guru Granth Sahib. What would it contain? *
2. Read the case studies and information in this unit, or watch the film clips. Then explain the importance of the Guru Granth Sahib, as if you were a journalist visiting to find out about how it's used and respected. Write up your notes into an article. ***
3. Write the speech that Guru Gobind Singh might have made to the Sikhs at the time, explaining why there will be no more human Gurus. **
4. In your opinion, do you think that religious believers could carry on with the strength of belief they have, without a holy scripture to read from? Explain your answer. **

2.6 The Faithful Followers: The Revelation of the Khalsa

1. Prepare an interview with the five Panj Piare, just after the end of the first Amrit ceremony in 1699. Think carefully about what questions to ask them – and even more carefully about what you think their answers might have been. **
2. Research the joining ceremonies of two other faiths and create a three-way Venn diagram to show their similarities and differences with Sikhism. **
3. If a person joins a faith, is it necessary to then take another step of commitment? What do you think this might give them? ***

Chapter 2 Assessment

Assessment in the *Student Book*

You will find an assessment task at the end of every chapter which focuses on AT2. In this chapter, the task asks students to create *A Little Book of Sikh Stories* suitable for use in RE lessons for children aged eight or nine.

In the *Student Book* (and on the supporting worksheets), you'll find guidance about levels of assessment that you can use to help your students understand what their work should include. You could ask them to use these criteria for self- or peer-assessment once they've completed the task.

Living Faiths Assessment

Student Book

- Assessment Task
- Levels Guidance

OxBox Online

- Auto-Marked Test
- Assessment Task Presentation
- Assessment Worksheets

Assessment Task for Chapter 2 (pages **30–31** of the *Sikhism Student Book*)

Objectives

- Examine the key people, places and events that contributed to the beliefs and practices of Sikhism, and present them in ways that enable others to understand their significance.
- Identify and re-tell stories that are important to Sikhs.

Task

Use the information about the key people, places and events in Sikhism in Chapter 2 to create *A Little Book of Sikh Stories* suitable for use in RE lessons for children aged eight or nine. Illustrate your cover and the stories in the book.

Assessment in *OxBox Online*

On the *Sikhism OxBox Online*, you'll find resources to use when introducing the assessment task to the class.

You can use the *Chapter 2 Assessment Task Presentation* as a front-of-class tool to help your students unpack the assessment criteria, and understand what is expected of them.

Chapter 2 Assessment Worksheets accompany the task, so that once you finish the presentation, your students can easily get started.

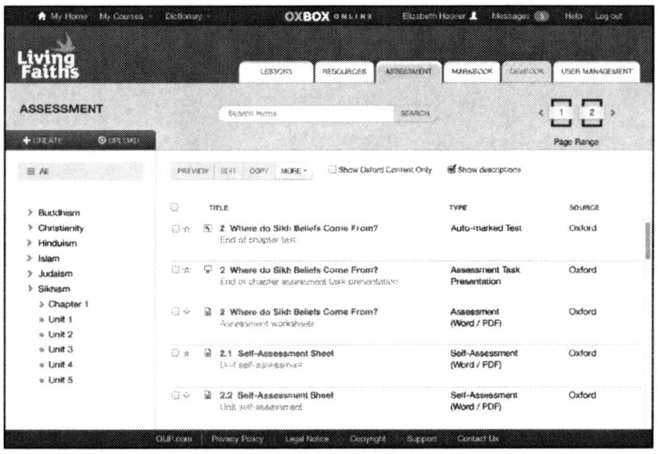

▲ Assessment resources for Chapter 2 on the *Sikhism Oxbox Online*

Auto-marked tests

The *Sikhism OxBox Online* also contains auto-marked tests for each chapter to help save you time setting questions and marking for AT1. The test for this chapter contains 15 questions and will take most students about half an hour. Test results are automatically stored in the markbook.

Digital markbook

A markbook and a reporting function complete the *OxBox Online* assessment package, so you can keep all your students' test results and assessment scores in one place. This can include the auto-marked tests as well as pieces of work you or the students have marked by hand.

Chapter 3 Overview
Belonging to the Sikh Faith

Helping you deliver Key Stage 3 RE

This chapter addresses the following areas of the Programme of Study:

Key concepts

Practices and ways of life

- Exploring the impact of religions and beliefs on how people live their lives
- Understanding that religious practices are diverse, change over time and are influenced by cultures

Expressing meaning

- Appreciating that individuals and cultures express their beliefs and values through many different forms

Key processes

Learning about religion

- Explain religious beliefs, practices and commitments, including their transmission by people, texts and traditions

Learning from religion

- Evaluate beliefs, commitments and the impact of religion in the contemporary world

The big picture

These are the key ideas behind this chapter:

- The Khalsa is the community of initiated Sikhs.
- The purpose of the Khalsa is to respect the poor, defend the weak, and understand that everyone is equal.
- Members of the Khalsa wear the Five Ks, which have a spiritual and symbolic significance.
- Sikhs conduct communal worship in the gurdwara, based around respect and veneration of the Guru Granth Sahib (the Sikh holy book).
- Sikhs acknowledge a number of different rites of passage, or Sanskars, each of which has its own rituals associated with it.
- Celebrating festivals together, such as Vaisakhi, is important to Sikhs.
- Service to the community, or seva, is a fundamental part of Sikhism. The langar plays an important role in this process, both practically and spiritually.

Chapter outline

Use this to give students a mental road map of the chapter:

3.1 Belonging to the Khalsa – explains what it means to belong to the Khalsa and shows how Khalsa Sikhs can be identified

3.2 What are the Five Ks? – uses case study examples to examine the significance of the Five Ks in more detail

3.3 Worship at the Gurdwara – explains the process of worship in a Sikh gurdwara

3.4 Journey of Life: Sikh Ceremonies – introduces the key rites of passage for Sikhs

3.5 Having Fun Remembering and Celebrating – discusses two key Sikh festivals and their significance in Sikh celebrations

3.6 What is So Important About Seva? – reflects on the key Sikh belief in service to the community as part of their faith

3.7 Food for Everybody – discusses in more depth the significance of the langar as part of Sikh service to the community

3.8 Should We Care For Others? – examines the Sikh duty of caring for others and giving both time and money to charity

Opportunities for assessment

Summative assessments on the *Sikhism OxBox Online* include automarked tests, interactive activities, and self-assessment worksheets.

The end-of-chapter assessment task in the *Student Book* provides formative assessment. Supporting materials for the assessment task can be found on the *Sikhism OxBox Online*, such as the Assessment Task Presentation and the related worksheets.

There are other opportunities for assessment too. For example, you could use some of the activities or reflection points throughout each *Student Book* unit, or some of the 'Further Suggestions' at the end of this chapter.

Getting ready for this chapter

- As this chapter covers worship at the gurdwara and the langar, you may wish to organize a trip to your local gurdwara if you have the resource, or invite a speaker to talk to the class.

- If you have the *Sikhism OxBox Online*, watch the case study film clips in advance, so that you can prepare and guide students before and during their viewing.

Objectives and outcomes for this chapter

Objectives	Unit	Outcomes
Most students will:		Most students will be able to:
• explain what it means to belong to the Khalsa • identify and explain the significance of the Five Ks • reflect on their own experiences of belonging.	**3.1**	• explain the purpose of the Khalsa • explain how a Sikh joins the Khalsa and what this commitment involves • consider what it means to belong.
• analyse and explain the deeper significance of the Five Ks • identify issues for Sikhs who wear the signs of their faith • reflect on their own responses to people who want to show the signs of their faith.	**3.2**	• discuss the significance and symbolism of the Five Ks in detail • acknowledge potential challenges between modern life and traditional Sikh practices • reflect on their own experiences of judging appearances.
• explain the role of the gurdwara • identify the significant elements of worship for a Sikh • reflect on the extent to which worship is a part of all lives.	**3.3**	• identify the place of the gurdwara in Sikhism • explain how worship takes place in a gurdwara • discuss the place of worship (not necessarily faith-based) in all lives.
• explain the key elements of the Sanskars • examine the importance of rituals in Sikh life • reflect on the importance of rituals in their own life.	**3.4**	• describe the four main Sikh rites of passage • explain the role of rituals in Sikhism • consider rituals in their own lives.
• explain the role and purpose of celebrating festivals in Sikhism • identify the impact on Sikhs of celebrating a festival • explore the values and celebrations within their own local community.	**3.5**	• discuss the history and significance of two main festivals in Sikhism • describe the impact on Sikhs of these celebrations • consider formal celebrations within their own community.
• explain what seva means and its importance for Sikhs • analyse the benefits of seva • reflect on their own feelings about serving others.	**3.6**	• explain the importance of service to the community in Sikhism • discuss what benefits service can bring • consider what the world would be like if everyone expressed selfless care for others.
• explain the significance of the langar in Sikhism • interpret the value of sharing and serving for Sikhs • reflect on ways of giving to their local community.	**3.7**	• explain that the langar is not just a place to eat, but has a deeper significance in Sikh beliefs • explain what spiritual benefits Sikhs gain from serving others • consider the possibilities of serving in relation to their own lives and community.
• explain Sikh teachings about how they should treat others • examine ways in which Sikhs give their time and money to help those in need • reflect on their own attitude towards caring for others.	**3.8**	• describe the key Sikh duty of giving to others – both time and money • explain practical ways in which Sikhs do this • consider their own attitudes towards caring for others, and what motivates them to do so.

3.1 Belonging to the Khalsa

The unit in brief

This unit uses a case study example to help examine why the Khalsa is so important in Sikhism, and what it means to a Sikh to be a part of it. It is an extension of Unit 2.6.

Key ideas

- The Khalsa is the community of initiated Sikhs who want to show a higher level of commitment to their faith
- Joining the Khalsa is a choice Sikhs make for themselves
- Sikhs join the Khalsa by taking part in an Amrit ceremony

Skills practised

- Thinking: explaining what the different physical elements of the Sikh faith might mean, based on previous learning
- Evaluation: evaluating the different levels of commitment that Sikhs can make within their faith
- Research: researching how other faiths indicate their sense of belonging
- Reflection: reflecting on what it means to belong

Resources

- 3.1 Khalsa Film Clip: Balwir Singh, a member of the Khalsa, talks about why he wears the Five Ks
- 3.1 Film Worksheet: students assess their understanding of the case study film clip by linking ideas to the
- 3.1 Khalsa Interactive Activity: students select true statements about what it means to belong to the Khalsa
- 3.1 Lesson Player: a ready-to-go presentation with built-in resources and teacher notes
- 3 Image Gallery: a useful gallery of photos and film stills from the chapter
- 3.1 Self-Assessment Sheet: students evaluate their learning against the lesson objectives

Ideas for starters

1. Use the Starter from the *Student Book*.
2. Ask students to use mini-whiteboards, or sheets of paper, to create a mini quiz for a partner based on their previous learning from Unit 2.6.
3. Ask students to create a series of badges that represent all the different things that they are proud to be a part of – even if it's just the human race!

Activity guidance

Many Sikhs choose to be part of the Khalsa, because they feel that it is the most important thing to do in Sikhism. However, there are many Sikhs who feel that they are just as committed to their faith, even though they choose not to follow the physical commitments of the Khalsa. This can be a delicate issue, so judge your class carefully when discussing this topic.

Ideas for plenaries

1. Use the Reflection from the *Student Book*.
2. Ask students: 'what does it mean to be "spiritually mature"?'
3. Ask students to go back to the unit's Learning Objectives and reflect on how well they think they have met them. Ask them to explain how they met them and what skills they think they have practised.
4. Refer to the photographs in the *Student Book* unit which show young Sikhs, and ask students to consider the question, 'how can you be an adult in your faith, when you are a teenager?'

Further class and homework activities

1. As homework, ask students to research a local Sikh community and make a presentation on how they interpret the evidence of the Khalsa in this community.
2. Ask students to use 3.1 Khalsa Interactive Activity on the to consolidate their learning about some of the key elements of the meaning and purpose of joining the Khalsa.
3. 3.1 Khalsa Film Clip on the .
4. 3.1 Film Worksheet on the .
5. Further suggestions on page 60 of this book.

3.2 What are the Five Ks?

The unit in brief

This unit uses case study quotations to look in more detail at what the Five Ks are, what they look like, and what they stand for. Students are also invited to consider the perspective of a Sikh who chooses not to wear the Five Ks.

Key ideas

- The Five Ks are: Kesh (uncut hair), Kachera (under-shorts), Kirpan (sword), Kangha (comb) and Kara (bracelet)
- Each of the Five Ks has a special meaning and symbolism, and Sikhs wear them to demonstrate love and respect for God
- Not all Sikhs choose to wear the Five Ks

Skills practised

- Thinking: considering the ways in which the Five Ks can have an impact on the life of Sikh
- Empathy: using analysis of the case study quotations to offer advice
- Reflection: reflecting on how appearance can influence reactions

Resources

- 3.2 Five Ks Film Clip: Balwir Singh explains why the Five Ks are significant for members of the Khalsa
- 3.2 Film Worksheet: students assess their understanding of the case study film clip by linking ideas to the *Student Book*
- 3.2 Five Ks Interactive Activity: students link each of the Five Ks with their explanations
- 3.2 Lesson Player: a ready-to-go presentation with built-in resources and teacher notes
- 3 Image Gallery: a useful gallery of photos and film stills from the chapter
- 3.2 Self-Assessment Sheet: students evaluate their learning against the lesson objectives

Ideas for starters

1. Use the Starter from the *Student Book*.
2. Revisit students' previous learning from Unit 3.1 by asking them to use mini-whiteboards, or similar, to create a word-cloud based on their learning from that unit.
3. If you have access to the Five Ks as artefacts, put them out and ask students to guess what they might represent – not what they are.

Activity guidance

The main point of this unit is to build on previous learning and explain that the Five Ks are important because of the meaning behind them. Aim to have students describing, reflecting on and evaluating these beliefs by the end of the lesson.

Ideas for plenaries

1. Use the Reflection from the *Student Book*.
2. Ask each student to choose a significant object that they could carry or wear every day to demonstrate their beliefs. They should explain their choice and also compare it to one of the Five Ks (the one they think is the most similar in meaning).
3. Complete a hot-seat exercise during which a student either volunteers, or is chosen, to sit as a Sikh at the front and answer suitable questions from the class.

Further class and homework activities

1. Ask students to look at the photo of Jatenderpal Singh in the *Student Book* (or on the board using 3 Image Gallery on the *Sikhism OxBox Online*) and write down three questions they would like to ask him about his experiences as a British soldier, linking it with his faith.
2. Ask students to use 3.2 Five Ks Interactive Activity on the *Sikhism OxBox Online* to consolidate their learning about the significance of the Five Ks.
3. As homework, ask students to research ways in which other faiths use external symbols to express their beliefs. Are they used for similar reasons to the Five Ks?
4. As another homework, ask students to create a short blog explaining their response to the following: 'Symbols without actions are pointless. Would you agree?'
5. 3.2 Five Ks Film Clip on the *Sikhism OxBox Online*.
6. 3.2 Film Worksheet on the *Sikhism OxBox Online*.
7. Further suggestions on page 60 of this book.

3.3 Worship at the Gurdwara

The unit in brief

This unit uses case study quotations to help explore how Sikhs worship at the gurdwara, and how the Guru Granth Sahib is used during worship.

Key ideas

- Sikhs worship at the gurdwara
- The Guru Granth Sahib is used during worship
- Worship plays an important role in a Sikh's life.

Useful Words

Chaur, Granthi, Gurbani, Palki, Sangat, Shabad, Takht

Skills practised

- Thinking: considering the impact of worship on the case study individuals
- Literacy: applying key words to an explanation
- Research: finding out how the Guru Granth Sahib is used in a Sikh home
- Reflection: reflecting on what people might worship

Resources

- 3.3 Gurdwara Film Clip A: Tohmev and Mr Singh describe how they worship at the gurdwara
- 3.3 Gurdwara Film Clip B: a guided tour of a gurdwara from UNITED SIKHS
- 3.3 Film Worksheet: students assess their understanding of the case study film clip by linking ideas to the *Student Book*
- 3.3 Worship Interactive Activity: students match key words about Sikh worship to their explanations
- 3.3 Lesson Player: a ready-to-go presentation with built-in resources and teacher notes
- 3 Image Gallery: a useful gallery of photos and film stills from the chapter
- 3.3 Self-Assessment Sheet: students evaluate their learning against the lesson objectives

Ideas for starters

1. Use the Starter from the .
2. Show images from this unit and ask students what they think the objects or processes are.
3. As a stilling exercise, play some Sikh tabla and harmonium music as students come into the room. Ask them to sit quietly for a few minutes while the music plays and then discuss how they felt.
4. Ask students to list as many different ways and places in which worship can happen as they can.

Activity guidance

Activity 3 in the *Student Book* asks students to research and compare how the Guru Granth Sahib is used at home and in the gurdwara. Encourage students to use images, annotation and the correct terminology in their work.

Ideas for plenaries

1. Use the Reflection from the *Student Book*.
2. Turn the whole classroom into a gurdwara and ask students to create all the different things present there. Get students to 'become' these things and then 'come to life' and explain themselves when asked – as a living installation.
3. Ask students, in pairs, to take turns saying a key word or phrase from this unit for their partner to explain (what it is and/or why it's important).
4. Ask students to create a definition for 'worship'.

Further class and homework activities

1. Ask students to put together a short role-play on the many different ways in which things can be 'worshipped' by humans. Share as a class, referring to the Reflection in the *Student Book*.
2. Ask students to use 3.3 Worship Interactive Activity on the *Sikhism OxBox Online* to consolidate their learning about worship at the gurdwara.
3. 3.3 Gurdwara Film Clips A and B on the *Sikhism OxBox Online*.
4. 3.3 Film Worksheet on the *Sikhism OxBox Online*.
5. Further suggestions on page 60 of this book.

3.4 Journey of Life: Sikh Ceremonies

The unit in brief

This unit is about the four main Sanskars, or rites of passage, in Sikhism. Each one is seen as more than a rite of passage by Sikhs; they are steps in their relationship and journey with God.

Key ideas

- Sanskars are rites of passage that mark key stages of life for Sikhs
- The four most important Sanskars are: Janam Naam Sanskar (the naming ceremony), Amrit Sanskar (the initiation ceremony), Anand Sanskar (the marriage ceremony), Antam Sanskar (the funeral ceremony)

Skills practised

- Literacy: analysing and rewriting a quotation from scripture
- Thinking: considering what rituals it might be necessary for all humans to be part of
- Reflection: reflecting on the importance of marking certain rites of passage

Resources

- 3.4 Mother's Blessing Audio Clip: a recording of the Mother's Blessing from the Guru Granth Sahib, page 496
- 3.4 Sanskars Worksheet: students answer questions about the Sanskars
- 3.4 Sanskars Interactive Activity: students fill the gaps in a paragraph about the Sanskars
- 3.4 Lesson Player: a ready-to-go presentation with built-in resources and teacher notes
- 3 Image Gallery: a useful gallery of photos and film stills from the chapter
- 3.4 Self-assessment Sheet: students evaluate their learning against the lesson objectives

Ideas for starters

1. Use the Starter from the *Student Book*.
2. Ask students to line up as a human continuum and imagine what key events they might be representing in a person's life. The first person would be the baby and the last would represent death and so on.
3. Encourage students to fill up the board with as many rites of passage and key events in a person's life as they can think of.

Activity guidance

- The starter in the *Student Book* could be extended with the question, 'what are you most/least looking forward to and why?'
- Activity 3 in the *Student Book*, which focuses on two rituals for all humans to go through, could end with fairly shallow responses. Stop students occasionally to see where they have got to in their thinking and direct them if necessary.

Ideas for plenaries

1. Use the Reflection from the *Student Book*.
2. Ask students to create chapter headings for the book of their life. What would they like the headings to be after reflecting on their learning in this unit?
3. Using mini-whiteboards or paper, ask students to take it in turns to explain what each Sanskar is and, more importantly, why it is significant in the life of a Sikh.
4. Go back to the human continuum line from Starter 2. What, if anything, would they change? What would they give a particular focus to?
5. Ask students to think back to their responses to the Starter in the *Student Book*. Which significant life events are still to come? Discuss and share – is there diversity in what they identify as key life events?
6. 'Whether we're religious or not, we need to mark stages of life in a special way.' Ask students whether they agree with this statement. Why or why not?

Further class and homework activities

1. Ask students to produce a class display board entitled 'Hopes and Aspirations', which is covered with the rites of passages and key events that they hope to go through.
2. Ask students to interview a parent or guardian about an event in their life that they considered to be a rite of passage. What happened, when, who was involved, what did it mean for them? Are there any similarities or differences with the few main Sanskars?
3. 3.4 Mother's Blessing Audio Clip on the *Sikhism OxBox Online*.
4. 3.4 Sanskars Worksheet on the *Sikhism OxBox Online*.
5. 3.4 Sanskars Interactive Activity on the *Sikhism OxBox Online*.
6. Further suggestions on page 60 of this book.

3.5 Having Fun Remembering and Celebrating

The unit in brief

This unit looks at the ways in which Sikhs celebrate key festivals in the UK, in particular Guru Nanak's Gurpurab and Vaisakhi.

Key ideas

- Two important Sikh celebrations are Guru Nanak's Gurpurab and Vaisakhi
- Guru Nanak's Gurpurab is when Sikhs celebrate the birth of Guru Nanak
- Vaisakhi, also known as Khalsa Day, is when Sikhs celebrate the revelation of the Khalsa

Useful Words

jakara, mela, Nagar Kirtan

Skills practised

- Literacy: writing a diary entry as a Sikh
- Research: finding out more about Guru Nanak's Gurpurab
- Reflection: reflecting on the part played by celebrations in the lives of those without a faith

Resources

- 3.5 Vaisakhi Worksheet: students look at an image and then answer questions on Vaisakhi
- 3.5 Festivals Interactive Activity: students match key terms from the unit with their definitions
- 3.5 Lesson Player: a ready-to-go presentation with built-in resources and teacher notes
- 3 Image Gallery: a useful gallery of photos and film stills from the chapter
- 3.5 Self-assessment Sheet: students evaluate their learning against the lesson objectives

Ideas for starters

1. Use the Starter from the *Student Book*.
2. Ask students to think of all the different local and national celebrations that people take part in.
3. Extend Starter 2 by discussing the impact that these different celebrations might have on individuals and communities.

4. Ask students which events they celebrate in their own lives. Ask what they do as part of the celebration – both as a community and in the home.
5. Ask students what traditions happen at any religious festivals they can name.

Activity guidance

- Celebrations like Vaisakhi are important for Sikhs, because they reinforce their cultural and religious identity as part of the worldwide Sikh community. This is important to emphasize to students, and can be part of any discussions about celebrations and festivals that students take part in.
- To support Activity 3 in the *Student Book*, which is about the importance of festivals in different faiths, you could refer to Unit 3.2 in the *Hindusim Student Book*, Unit 2.5 in the *Buddhism Student Book*, and Units 3.4–3.5 in the *Judaism Student Book*.

Ideas for plenaries

1. Use the Reflection from the *Student Book*.
2. Ask students to come up with their own question arising from this unit. Choose a student to begin by asking another student their question. That second student has to answer the first question and then ask a third student their own question, and so on.
3. Ask students to create an emotions board, which they feel reflects the emotions that Sikhs might go through during Vaisakhi.
4. Ask students whether they agree with the following statement: 'Festivals unite communities in identity. Every community should celebrate what it stands for.'

Further class and homework activities

1. Ask students to use 3.5 Vaisakhi Worksheet on the *Sikhism OxBox Online* to guide their research.
2. Ask students to use 3.5 Festivals Interactive Activity on the *Sikhism OxBox Online* to demonstrate their understanding of Sikh celebrations.
3. 'It is important to celebrate festivals in the same way year after year.' Ask students to show agreement/disagreement with this statement. How would a Sikh respond? What other examples can students give from faiths they have studied to show the importance of celebrating festivals annually?
4. Further suggestions on page 60 of this book.

3.6 What is So Important About Seva?

The unit in brief

This unit uses case study examples to discuss what seva is, why Sikhs perform it, and how it can contribute to the community. It also explores the idea of simran (meditating on God).

Key ideas

- Seva, or sewa, is selfless service and is very important in Sikhism
- There are three main types of service: tan (physical service), man (mental service), dhan (giving to charity)

Useful Words

langar, simran

Skills practised

- Thinking: considering different examples of seva which Sikhs could do to help their local communities
- Literacy: defining and applying a word in context
- Reflection: reflecting on how helping people might make the world a better place

Resources

- 3.6 Seva Audio Clip: a recording of a quotation about seva from the Guru Granth Sahib, pages 25–26
- 3.6 Langar Film Clip: Mrs Kaur, Baltej and Mr Singh discuss how Sikhs can do seva at the langar in their gurdwara
- 3.6 Film Worksheet: students assess their understanding of the case study film clip by linking ideas to the *Student Book*
- 3.6 Langar Interactive Activity: students fill the gaps in a paragraph about the langar
- 3.6 Lesson Player: a ready-to-go presentation with built-in resources and teacher notes
- 3 Image Gallery: a useful gallery of photos and film stills from the chapter
- 3.6 Self-assessment Sheet: students evaluate their learning against the lesson objectives

Ideas for starters

1. Use the Starter from the *Student Book*.
2. Divide the class into two groups (maybe with coloured dots handed out at random as they come in). Ask one group to serve the other with food and drink before getting some for themselves and sitting on the floor. Ask students to reflect on how it felt to be server or served.

3. Ask students to imagine that they can either have servants, or have the chance to serve those most in need. Ask which they would choose and why.
4. Ask students to consider which forms of paid and unpaid service they would be prepared to do. Ask for reasons.

Activity guidance

Seva and simran combine together to give Sikhs spiritual balance in life. Try to bring this balance out in the activities and discussions that you have, and come back to it regularly, because it will help students to find greater understanding in the themes that are coming up.

Ideas for plenaries

1. Use the Reflection from the *Student Book*.
2. Get a small group of students to come up to the front and give them 30 seconds each to recap what they have learned and what skills they have practised as part of this unit. Ask the remaining students to pick up on anything they have left out.
3. Get students to repeat Starter 2 above. Ask who wants to serve and who wants to be served. Have any students' views changed as a result of the work in this lesson?
4. If students had to perform some kind of service for others, ask them what they would choose to do and why.
5. Ask students to think about the Guru Granth Sahib quotation in the *Student Book*. How might giving selfless service to others bring peace to the person who is doing it?

Further class and homework activities

1. Ask students to consider the possibility of a 'service based' activity for your school to develop, either for other students in school or the local community. How might Sikh values help to develop the idea? Put together a plan to carry it out.
2. Ask students to use 3.6 Langar Interactive Activity on the *Sikhism OxBox Online* to consolidate their learning about the langar.
3. 3.6 Langar Film Clip on the *Sikhism OxBox Online*.
4. 3.6 Seva Audio Clip on the *Sikhism OxBox Online*.
5. 3.6 Film Worksheet on the *Sikhism OxBox Online*.
6. Further suggestions on page 60 of this book.

3.7 Food for Everybody

The unit in brief

This unit uses case study examples to explore the day-to-day running of the langar, why it's there, who it's for, and what it can bring to Sikh individuals and communities, plus the wider community.

Key ideas

- The langar is the name given to the food and the room where it's served in a gurdwara
- The langar exists to serve the wider community
- Equality plays an important part in the ethos of the langar

Skills practised

- Empathy: imagining themselves in the positions of the case study participants
- Thinking: applying the principles of the langar to the content of photos
- Reflection: reflecting on why sharing food is so important in many faiths

Resources

- 3.7 Langar Film Clip A: Mrs Kaur, Baltej and Mr Singh discuss how Sikhs can do seva at the langar in their gurdwara
- 3.7 Langar Film Clip B: Balwir Singh discusses the langar at his gurdwara
- 3.7 Film Worksheet: students assess their understanding of the case study film clips by linking ideas to the *Student Book*
- 3.7 Langar Interactive Activity: students select true statements about why the langar is significant in Sikhism
- 3.7 Lesson Player: a ready-to-go presentation with built-in resources and teacher notes
- 3 Image Gallery: a useful gallery of photos and film stills from the chapter
- 3.7 Self-assessment Sheet: students evaluate their learning against the lesson objectives

Ideas for starters

1. Use the Starter from the *Student Book*.
2. Show the two photos from the right-hand page of this unit (if you have access to the *Sikhism OxBox Online*, you could use 3 Image Gallery to do this). Then ask students to imagine that they are the people shown in the pictures. Ask what they would be giving or gaining in those moments.
3. Recap on previous work by asking students what they have already learned about the langar and its role in previous units.

Activity guidance

The photos in this unit demonstrate the langar uniting a diverse group of people in one room, reinforcing the principles of equality and service. As an extension of the related activity, you could ask students to research, design or draw an illustration to reflect the global community that Sikhs see themselves as part of.

Ideas for plenaries

1. Use the Reflection from the *Student Book*.
2. Ask students, working in small groups, to decide on a number of sentences that summarize their learning and achievement over the last few units. They then have to work out a way to present them without saying a word.
3. Ask students to decide whether or not they have met this unit's Learning Objectives. If they have, how and if not, what do they need to do.
4. Ask students to use key words and phrases to create an acroshic poem about the langar, using the word LANGAR.

Further class and homework activities

1. Ask students to design an invite to everyone in your local community that they think would benefit from being part of the langar.
2. Ask students to use 3.7 Langar Interactive Activity on the *Sikhism OxBox Online* to consolidate their learning about the langar.
3. 3.7 Langar Film Clips A and B on the *Sikhism OxBox Online*.
4. 3.7 Film Worksheet on the *Sikhism OxBox Online*.
5. Further suggestions on page 60 of this book.

3.8 Should We Care For Others?

The unit in brief

This unit considers the principles of dhan, vand chhakna and daswandh, which are all teachings about caring and giving – both time and money – to those in need. It also examines a particular Sikh charity that aims to support these principles and help those in great need.

Key ideas

- There is a Sikh duty to care for others
- Sikhs give time and money to charity
- The duty of daswandh is when Sikhs give a tenth of their salary as a charitable donation

Skills practised

- Thinking: considering whether or not caring and giving is something innate to us
- Research: finding out more about Khalsa Aid and its founder
- Reflection: suggesting responses to whether or not we have a responsibility to care for those in need

Resources

- 3.8 Challenge Cards Worksheet: students design cards to challenge others about those in need around the world
- 3.8 Caring for Others Interactive Activity: students link key words from this unit with their explanations
- 3.8 Lesson Player: a ready-to-go presentation with built-in resources and teacher notes
- 3 Image Gallery: a useful gallery of photos and film stills from the chapter
- 3.8 Self-assessment Sheet: students evaluate their learning against the lesson objectives

Ideas for starters

1. Use the Starter from the *Student Book*.
2. Write on the board: 'You must give away 10% of your earnings to people you do not know.' Ask students for their reactions to this. What questions do they need to ask before they can answer fully?
3. Extend Starter 2 by explaining that the money will go to those who are in dire need. Does it change students' initial responses?

Activity guidance

Remind students about the work they have already completed on the Khalsa, plus any teachings and ideas on the pages of this unit, before they complete the activity about Khalsa Aid and its founder. You'll need access to ICT for students to complete their research.

Ideas for plenaries

1. Use the Reflection from the *Student Book*.
2. Ask students, in pairs or small groups, to have a debate using the Reflection in the *Student Book*.
3. Ask students to suggest ways in which dhan could be demonstrated in school. Are there any students who would be prepared to put these into practice?
4. If giving was a duty for all of those who could, ask students how much they think should be given.

Further class and homework activities

1. As homework, ask students to find a newspaper or news website and look for stories which show examples of how people show care for others. They should be prepared to share and discuss their findings.
2. Ask students to think of the different ways they can show care to:

   a) their friends and family

   b) other people they do not know.
3. 3.8 Challenge Cards Worksheet on the *Sikhism OxBox Online*.
4. 3.8 Caring for Others Interactive Activity on the *Sikhism OxBox Online*.
5. Further suggestions on page 60 of this book.

Chapter 3 Further Suggestions

These suggestions are addressed directly to students.

3.1 Belonging to the Khalsa

1. Why do you think Sikhs find so much joy in belonging to the Khalsa? *
2. Think about the countries and areas in need that you are aware of and put together a role-play that shows what contribution you think the Khalsa could make to these areas. ***
3. Plan, prepare and perform a short film on the benefit of belonging. **

3.2 What are the Five Ks?

1. Create a poster that answers the title question of the unit. *
2. Create a list of commitments you have, and the ones you would like to have, and order them according to importance. *
3. As a class, get into groups of 2–3, and your teacher will allocate each one a different 'K'. Prepare information about it and then 1–2 members of the group should go round the others to learn about theirs whilst the last member stays to teach those who come over. In the end, everyone regroups to teach or learn what they have gathered. **
4. The Five Ks are objects that represent much more than you see. Create a leaflet or manifesto that explains what you would be prepared to wear to represent your beliefs. **

3.3 Worship at the Gurdwara

1. Go, as a class, to your local gurdwara and watch the worship take place. Note the ways in which the Guru Granth Sahib is used during worship. **
2. Watch the *Sikhism OxBox Online* videos of how the Guru Granth Sahib is used at home (or find videos online) and, imagining you are a journalist, write an article on the meaning and importance of the Guru Granth Sahib in this context. **
3. Make a model of the prayer hall in the gurdwara, annotating all the different elements and why they are significant for Sikhs – explaining their meaning and symbolism. ***

3.4 The Journey of Life

1. Create a diagram in your book, using key words and symbols, which demonstrates each of the Sanskars. **
2. Explain the importance of the Sanskars as if you were a journalist. Write up your notes on this unit into an article. **
3. Write the speech that a parent might give to their child as part of the ceremony when they take Amrit for the first time. *
4. In your opinion, do you think religious belief would be as strong if there were no ceremonies or communities to be part of? ***

3.5 Having Fun Remembering and Celebrating

1. Create your own festival as a class. What would you celebrate? How does it compare to a Sikh festival? *
2. Film a mock television interview with a family who are celebrating on the streets as part of the Nagar Kirtan. **
3. Put together the resources needed for an entire display board about Sikh celebrations. Think about the colours and designs you'll need. **
4. Design a flag for a real celebration that exists (look at the Nishan Sahib for inspiration). *

3.6 What is So Important About Seva?

1. Find out more about seva and how Sikhs perform it. Make a list and use images and symbols to illustrate the list. *
2. Film an interview with people in the langar who are visitors. Imagine what their experience would be like. Alternatively, visit a langar and film each other afterwards talking about your experiences. **
3. Do you think it is necessary to help others if you follow a faith? Isn't faith an internal thing? Respond to this using a method of your choice. ***

3.7 Food for Everybody

1. Research the ways in which different faiths help others and create a word cloud to show the similarities and differences. **
2. Create a seva and langar board game – think carefully about all the things that could be included to demonstrate your learning. ***
3. As a class, make a langar meal and serve it to the rest of your year or the teachers! *

3.8 Should We Care For Others?

1. Use the information in this unit, and conduct your own research, to prepare a short presentation for an assembly on 'Caring for Others'. Explain why a Sikh would think it is important to support a charity helping people suffering from disease or hunger. **
2. Give examples from other faiths you have studied of beliefs and teachings about caring for others. What is their motivation? Consider the motivations of those who are not part of a religion, but who also believe it is important to care for others. What are the similarities and differences? ***

Chapter 3 Assessment

Assessment in the *Student Book*

You will find an assessment task at the end of every chapter which focuses on AT2. In this chapter, the task asks students to write a letter from a parent to a teenager who is getting ready to join the Khalsa.

In the *Student Book* (and on the supporting worksheets), you'll find guidance about levels of assessment that you can use to help your students understand what their work should include. You could ask them to use these criteria for self- or peer- assessment once they've completed the task.

Living Faiths Assessment

Student Book

- Assessment Task
- Levels Guidance

OxBox Online

- Auto-Marked Test
- Assessment Task Presentation
- Assessment Worksheets

Assessment Task for Chapter 3 (pages **48–49** of the *Sikhism Student Book*)

Objectives

- Explore and explain the ways in which faith can give more to a person than simply something to worship.
- Reflect on your own ideas about where guidance and direction can come from in life.

Task

Your task is to write a letter from a parent to a teenager, aged around 13–14, who is getting ready to join the Khalsa by having an Amrit ceremony. In the letter, explain:

- why the Khalsa is so important
- what it can give a Sikh in terms of support and guidance
- how the Five Ks can make a big difference to a Sikh's life.

Also refer to the greater responsibilities that the teenager will now have – especially in terms of seva and their own worship in the gurdwara.

Assessment in *OxBox Online*

On the *Sikhism OxBox Online*, you'll find resources to use when introducing the assessment task to the class.

You can use the *Chapter 3 Assessment Task Presentation* as a front-of-class tool to help your students unpack the assessment criteria, and understand what is expected of them.

Chapter 3 Assessment Worksheets accompany the task, so that once you finish the presentation, your students can easily get started.

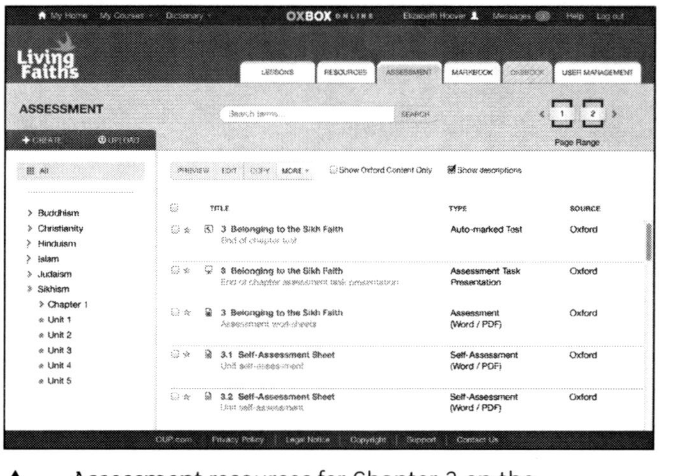

▲ Assessment resources for Chapter 3 on the *Sikhism Oxbox Online*

Auto-marked tests

The *Sikhism OxBox Online* also contains auto-marked tests for each chapter to help save you time setting questions and marking for AT1. The test for this chapter contains 15 questions and will take most students about half an hour. Test results are automatically stored in the markbook.

Digital markbook

A markbook and a reporting function complete the *OxBox Online* assessment package, so you can keep all your students' test results and assessment scores in one place. This can include the auto-marked tests as well as pieces of work you or the students have marked by hand.

Chapter 4 Overview
Raising Questions, Exploring Answers

Helping you deliver Key Stage 3 RE

This chapter addresses the following areas of the Programme of Study:

Key concepts

Beliefs, teachings and sources

- Understanding and responding critically to beliefs and attitudes

Meaning, purpose and truth

- Exploring some of the ultimate questions that confront humanity, and responding imaginatively to them

Values and commitments

- Understanding how moral values and a sense of obligation can come from beliefs and experience
- Evaluating their own and others' values in order to make informed, rational and imaginative choices

Key processes

Learning about religion

- Investigate the impact of religious beliefs and teachings on individuals, communities and societies, the reasons for commitment and the causes of diversity
- Evaluate how religious beliefs and teachings inform answers to ultimate questions and ethical issues

Learning from religion

- Reflect on the relationship between beliefs, teachings, world issues and ultimate questions
- Express insights into the significance and value of religion and other world views for human relationships
- Express their own beliefs and ideas, using a variety of forms of expression, including creative forms and reasoned arguments

The big picture

These are the key ideas behind this chapter:

- Sikhs believe that wealth should be used to help the poor and vulnerable.
- Because, according to Sikhism, the world was created by God, Sikhs believe that it's the duty of all humans to look after His creation.
- It is possible in Sikhism for both faith and science to work side by side without conflict.
- Sikhs believe that all life begins at conception, and that the divine spark of God is in everyone. Therefore, Sikhism finds issues such as abortion and euthanasia unacceptable in most instances. However, certain medical procedures, such as IVF, can be considered acceptable if there is no testing or destruction of embryos.
- Sikhs believe that the person who they will marry is already pre-ordained by God. Marriage is seen as a spiritual union between two equal partners.

Chapter outline

Use this to give students a mental road map of the chapter:

4.1 A Question of Money – uses the story of Duni Chand and Guru Nanak to discuss the role of money and wealth in Sikhism

4.2 Our Environment: Living in Harmony – examines the connections between Sikhism and care for the environment

4.3 Sikhism and Science: United or Divided? – begins to examine the relationship between Sikhism and science, explored further in Units 4.4 and 4.5

4.4 Matters of Life and Death: Abortion – uses Sikh beliefs about life and death to discuss the medical ethical issue of abortion

4.5 Medical Ethics: IVF and Cloning – considers medical ethical issues from a Sikh perspective

4.6 Friends? Relationships? Marriage? – examines Sikh attitudes towards relationships, both romantic and otherwise

Opportunities for assessment

Summative assessments on the *Sikhism OxBox Online* include automarked tests, interactive activities, and self-assessment worksheets.

The end-of-chapter assessment task in the *Student Book* provides formative assessment. Supporting materials for the assessment task can be found on the *Sikhism OxBox Online*, such as the Assessment Task Presentation and the related worksheets.

There are other opportunities for assessment too. For example, you could use some of the activities or reflection points throughout each *Student Book* unit, or some of the 'Further Suggestions' at the end of this chapter.

Getting ready for this chapter

- Students will probably have completed work on units that look at key teaching and themes in Sikhism, which will help them in their responses. If they haven't done as yet (or did so some time ago), it could be beneficial to spend a little time exploring or revisiting some of the basics from earlier chapters.
- This chapter and Chapter 5, in particular, require students to be able to explain and apply their own ideas and beliefs, so you could spend a lesson exploring a range of ethical issues and modern dilemmas to get them familiar with the types of questions they will be looking at.
- If you have the *Sikhism OxBox Online*, watch the case study film clips in advance, so that you can prepare and guide students before and during their viewing.

Objectives and outcomes for this chapter

Objectives	Unit	Outcomes
Most students will:		Most students will be able to:
• examine the story of Duni Chand and the lesson it offers for Sikhs • explore the role of wealth and the desire for it in the modern world • reflect on their own approach to money.	**4.1**	• explain the moral of the story of Duni Chand • describe Sikh beliefs about the role of wealth • consider whether or not others should be helped only when they ask for help.
• explain Sikh beliefs about the relationship between humans and the environment • identify some environmental ethical issues and how Sikhs respond to them • reflect on taking responsibility for the environment.	**4.2**	• describe the connections between the creation of the planet by God and the responsibility of humans to look after it • consider how Sikhs would react to certain environmental issues • consider whether we have a responsibility to look after the environment for future generations.
• examine the relationship between Sikhism and science • compare the approaches of a Sikh and a scientist to our universe • reflect on where they stand in terms of these two approaches.	**4.3**	• explain why Sikhism and science are not necessarily in conflict • consider, in particular, the two approaches to the origins of the universe • consider their personal perspective.
• explain Sikh attitudes towards abortion • analyse Sikh teaching about the sanctity of human life • reflect on their own views about the issues raised.	**4.4**	• describe and explain the Sikh attitude towards ending a life through either abortion or euthanasia • explain the Sikh views about the sanctity of life • evaluate their personal perspective.
• explain Sikh attitudes to IVF and cloning • analyse Sikh teachings about the sanctity of human life • reflect on their own views about the issues raised.	**4.5**	• describe Sikh attitudes towards medical ethical issues such as IVF and cloning • consider their personal perspective on whether every human and animal has a soul.
• explain how some Sikhs view friendships • analyse Sikh attitudes towards marriage • reflect on their own friendships and the relationships around them.	**4.6**	• discuss and explain Sikh attitudes towards friendships • explain Sikh attitudes towards marriage and God's role within it • consider their personal perspective on dating and singleness.

4.1 A Question of Money

The unit in brief

This unit explores Sikh attitudes towards money, as expressed through the story of Duni Chand. This is one of the stories from Guru Nanak's life. It also aims to allow students to compare and contrast it with their own attitudes towards money and gaining wealth.

Key ideas

- Sikhism offers a perspective on why people desire money
- Guru Nanak taught his followers about how to respond to money and the desire for wealth
- A person cannot take their wealth with them when they die

Skills practised

- Literacy: putting the story of Duni Chand into their own words
- Thinking: applying the situation to themselves and to Sikhs
- Reflection: reflecting on our responsibility for others in need

Resources

- 4.1 Wealth Audio Clip: a recording about wealth from the Guru Granth Sahib, page 268
- 4.1 Duni Chand Worksheet: students create a visual representation of what Duni Chand was trying to hold on to
- 4.1 Duni Chand Interactive Activity: students link sentence starters about Duni Chand with their endings
- 4.1 Lesson Player: a ready-to-go presentation with built-in resources and teacher notes
- 4 Image Gallery: a useful gallery of photos and film stills from the chapter
- 4.1 Self-Assessment Sheet: students evaluate their learning against the lesson objectives

Ideas for starters

1. Use the Starter from the *Student Book*.
2. Ask students to imagine that they are friends with someone who has just won the Lottery – but their friend doesn't give them any of their winnings. Ask them if they think they should be given something. Would the money change their friendship? Is having money more important than having friends?
3. As students come into the class, give some of them a 'million pound note' and others nothing. Then separate the class into those that have a million pounds and those that don't. Say to those with the money that they need to plan how they are going to spend it.

Hand a sticky note to those who don't have any money and say that they can write what they would like on it. After a while, bring the two groups back together and compare what they came up with. What positive or negative things have come up?

4. Ask the class to imagine that they are in charge of the country, and explain that their first task is to achieve more of a balance with the money that exists. They have to decide who they are going to take money from, and who they are going to give money to, in order to make things fairer.

Activity guidance

If you choose to do Starter 2 above (and/or Plenaries 3 and 4 below), you will need to create some 'million pound notes' beforehand, to hand out to selected students as they enter the lesson.

Ideas for plenaries

1. Use the Reflection from the *Student Book*.
2. Ask students to consider whether Duni Chand was helping others when he gave up all his money, or whether he was helping himself. Ask whether it is ever possible to do something for another person without gaining something yourself.
3. If you started with the million pound note activity above (Starter 2), ask students to pick them up again. Ask them whether they would change anything about their original choices. Why/why not?
4. If you didn't start with the million pound notes, give them out now. Ask what each student would do with them. Would they make it all about material goods, or would they work on their personal development too?
5. Say to the class that tomorrow is 'Duni Chand Day'. Ask what they could do to celebrate it. What would Guru Nanak recommend?

Further class and homework activities

1. Ask students to design an event that encourages young people away from money and towards more altruistic and selfless activities.
2. Ask students to write to themselves, explaining what their attitude is towards money, and whether or not it needs to change.
3. Ask students to create 'before' and 'after' interviews with Duni Chand.
4. 4.1 Wealth Audio Clip on the *Sikhism OxBox Online*.
5. 4.1 Duni Chand Worksheet on the *Sikhism OxBox Online*.
6. 4.1 Duni Chand Interactive Activity on the *Sikhism OxBox Online*.
7. Further suggestions on page 76 of this book.

4.2 Our Environment: Living in Harmony

The unit in brief

This unit explores Sikh attitudes towards the natural world and environmental issues. Sikhs believe that they have a responsibility to care for the environment, and respect all that it gives them.

Key ideas

- Sikh beliefs about the origins of the world affect their approach to environmental issues
- Sikhs support a range of environmental causes and organizations, including Sikh Environment Day and EcoSikh

Useful Words

biodiversity, harmony, sustainable

Skills practised

- Literacy: interpreting and analysing an EcoSikh quotation; creating a flier, writing a role-play; writing a radio report
- Thinking: considering Sikh views to a specific environmental issue
- Reflection: reflecting on our generation's responsibility for the natural world

Resources

- 4.2 Environment Worksheet: students complete a job application for a job with a Sikh environment action group
- 4.2 Environment Interactive Activity: students fill the gaps in a paragraph on Sikh beliefs about the environment
- 4.2 Lesson Player: a ready-to-go presentation with built-in resources and teacher notes
- 4 Image Gallery: a useful gallery of photos and film stills from the chapter
- 4.2 Self-Assessment Sheet: students evaluate their learning against the lesson objectives

Ideas for starters

1. Use the Starter from the *Student Book*.
2. Give students up to five minutes with a partner/group to jot down as many environmental issues as they can. Randomly pick a small selection of students who then have to speak for one minute on one of the issues identified.
3. Play 'Teacher hot-seat'. Allow students 10–20 questions to try to find out what the topic/objective is for this lesson.
4. Give each student a sticky note, on which they have to write down secretly the effect or cause of an environmental issue – before

sticking it to their partner's forehead without them reading it. The pair should then play 'yes or no' to figure out what is written on each sticky note.

5. Before the lesson, write the following quote on the board (without any context): 'If you knew something could be done to prevent something terrible happening, would you do it?' Then ask students what they think.
6. Find out and list all the things that the students in your class do to care for the environment.

Activity guidance

Activity 1 in the *Student Book* might require some initial teacher guidance about the level at which to pitch the flier for Year 2 and 3 students.

Ideas for plenaries

1. Use the Reflection from the *Student Book*.
2. 'Any action by an individual is merely a drop in the ocean. There is no point in even trying.' Take a class vote on this, asking for reasons and references to what students have learned in the lesson.
3. Get the class to work as a group and choose a word/phrase related to what they have learned from the lesson for each letter of the alphabet. So 'A' could be 'animal extinction', 'B' could be 'biodiversity' and so on.

Further class and homework activities

1. Ask students to create a flow chart that shows the origins of Sikh beliefs about the environment, including how/why they act to protect it.
2. Ask students, individually or in small groups, to create an advert that encourages action about an environmental problem – using the Sikh beliefs and responses they have studied in this unit.
3. As homework, ask students to write to themselves explaining their attitude to the environment and whether or not it needs to change.
4. As another homework, ask students to write a magazine article that contains interviews with a Sikh and the manager of an oilrig. Ask them to compare and contrast their ideas in the article's summary.
5. 4.2 Environment Worksheet on the *Sikhism OxBox Online*.
6. 4.2 Environment Interactive Activity on the *Sikhism OxBox Online*.
7. Further suggestions on page 76 of this book.

4.3 Sikhism and Science: United or Divided?

The unit in brief

This unit uses case study quotations to help examine ways in which Sikhism responds to the developments and progress of science, in particular beliefs held about the origins of the universe.

Key ideas

- Many people argue that science and religion are in constant conflict
- Scientists have theories (for example, the Big Bang) to explain the origins of the universe, whilst faiths usually believe that a divine being created the universe
- Many Sikhs believe that these scientific theories are compatible with their beliefs about God

Useful Words

Big Bang, Gurmukhs

Skills practised

- Evaluation: evaluating whether or not Sikhism and science do have clear links
- Literacy: writing an explanatory email from a Sikh to a Humanist friend
- Reflection: reflecting on the possible impacts of belief in a creator

Resources:

- 4.3 Universe Audio Clip: a recording of quotations about the universe from the Guru Granth Sahib, pages 1, 3, 4 and 276
- 4.3 Sikhism and Science Film Clip: Mejindarpal Kaur discusses the relationship between Sikh and scientific beliefs about creation
- 4.3 Film Worksheet: students assess their understanding of the case study film clip by linking ideas to the *Student Book*
- 4.3 Sikhism and Science Interactive Activity: students decide whether statements about Sikhism and science are true or false
- 4.3 Lesson Player: a ready-to-go presentation with built-in resources and teacher notes
- 4 Image Gallery: a useful gallery of photos and film stills from the chapter
- 4.3 Self-Assessment Sheet: students evaluate their learning against the lesson objectives

Ideas for starters

1. Use the Starter from the *Student Book*.
2. Ask students to consider what they have already learned about Sikh beliefs and to apply it to this unit. What do they think the response of Sikhism to science might be?

Activity guidance

- Once students have completed the continuum task in the *Student Book*, get the whole class up and create a class continuum – choosing students to justify and compare their choices.
- For Activity 3 in the *Student Book*, you may need to clarify with students what a Humanist might believe. Humanism does not uphold or support religious or supernatural beliefs. It seeks to promote human reason, ethics and justice.

Ideas for plenaries

1. Use the Reflection from the *Student Book*.
2. Ask students to role-play, in small groups, a news item in which the reporter goes looking for the response of Sikhs to recent scientific developments.
3. Ask students to create a flow chart that shows how Sikhs think that their beliefs intertwine with science.
4. Introduce students to the idea that the universe is fundamentally linked to humanity and how we see ourselves. Many scientists are preoccupied with understanding the workings of the universe. Are Sikhs (and those of other faiths you have studied) trying to find answers to the same questions as scientists? How? Discuss ideas.

Further class and homework activities

1. As a possible starter, show 4.3 Sikhism and Science Film Clip on the *Sikhism OxBox Online* to the class. Ask students to choose six words or phrases from the film clip that they feel might be significant for this topic.
2. Ask students to use 4.3 Sikhism and Science Interactive Activity on the *Sikhism OxBox Online* to demonstrate their understanding of the links between Sikhism and science.
3. 4.3 Universe Audio Clip on the *Sikhism OxBox Online*.
4. 4.3 Film Worksheet on the *Sikhism OxBox Online*.
5. Further suggestions on page 76 of this book.

4.4 Matters of Life and Death: Abortion

The unit in brief

This unit concentrates on the key ethical issue of abortion, considering teachings and guidance from Sikhism and the Gurus about the sanctity of human life. It also encourages students to reflect on where they stand on this issue.

Key ideas

- Medical ethics involves deciding what is right and wrong when providing treatment which could save, improve or end a life
- Sikhs believe that life begins at conception, and that the divine spark of God is in everyone
- Sikhs believe that only God can decide when a soul should die, which means that issues such as abortion, embryo testing and euthanasia raise difficult questions for Sikhs

Useful Words

abortion, conception, embryo testing, euthanasia, sacred

Skills practised

- Thinking: considering arguments about when life begins
- Literacy: writing a convincing speech; analysing and rewording quotations
- Research: researching and comparing ideas with those of a Humanist or member of another faith
- Reflection: reflecting on the possible dangers of humans playing God

Resources

- 4.4 Sorting Worksheet: students create a set of sorting cards to help them create an argument about an issue of medical ethics
- 4.4 Abortion Interactive Activity: students decide whether statements about abortion are true or false
- 4.4 Lesson Player: a ready-to-go presentation with built-in resources and teacher notes
- 4 Image Gallery: a useful gallery of photos and film stills from the chapter
- 4.4 Self-Assessment Sheet: students evaluate their learning against the lesson objectives

Ideas for starters

1. Use the Starter from the *Student Book*.
2. Create a mind-map about medical ethics, with the challenge of filling the board with the class's ideas.
3. Ask students to spend ten minutes researching medical ethics, with the objective of finding a set of quotes to show the different approaches that people can take.

Activity guidance

- The subject of abortion is a sensitive one, so you may decide to ask for student volunteers when personal opinions have to be given.
- You could compare Sikh attitudes to abortion with those of another faith. See Unit 4.2 in the *Christianity Student Book*.

Ideas for plenaries

1. Use the Reflection from the *Student Book*.
2. Ask a student volunteer to explain the Sikh approach towards abortion, followed by their own opinion. Then ask another student volunteer to say whether or not they agree with the first student's opinion and, if not, why not. They should then give a different Sikh view. Carry on in this way (not always insisting on links to Sikhism).
3. Try to go through the alphabet with the class to summarize the lesson. For example, A is for abortion, B for birth, etc.
4. Get one or two of the students to come up to the front and explain what the lesson has been about, using the unit's Learning Objectives.
5. Use Activity 4 in the *Student Book* to hold a class debate.

Further class and homework activities

1. Ask students to use 4.4 Sorting Worksheet on the *Sikhism OxBox Online* to create a set of sorting cards about a medical ethical issue.
2. Ask students to use 4.4 Abortion Interactive Activity on the *Sikhism OxBox Online* to demonstrate their knowledge about medical ethical issues.
3. Further suggestions on page 76 of this book.

4.5 Medical Ethics: IVF and Cloning

The unit in brief

This unit makes use of case study quotations to examine more issues about medical ethics, including IVF and cloning. A case study family shares how Sikhs would respond to these controversial issues. Students are encouraged to think about their own opinions.

Key ideas

- Important medical ethical issues include IVF, animal testing, and cloning
- There are principles within Sikhism relevant to the above issues, though the Guru Granth Sahib does not refer to them directly
- Sikhs use the Guru Granth Sahib to interpret complex issues for themselves

Useful Words

cloning, IVF

Skills practised

- Empathy: considering the feelings of a Sikh couple who are unable to conceive
- Research: researching and explaining more about what is involved in IVF
- Reflection: reflecting on personal opinions about these medical ethical issues; considering whether every human and animal has a soul
- Analysis: exploring arguments given by Sikhism and Sikhs about these issues

Resources

- 4.5 Medical Ethics Film Clip A: the Singh/Kaur family talk about how Sikh teachings help them to make difficult decisions about medical ethics, such as IVF
- 4.5 Medical Ethics Film Clip B: the Singh/Kaur family talk about abortion
- 4.5 Medical Ethics Film Clip C: the Singh/Kaur family talk about animal testing and cloning
- 4.5 Film Worksheet: students assess their understanding of the case study film clips by linking ideas to the *Student Book*
- 4.5 Medical Ethics Interactive Activity: students fill the gaps in a paragraph on Sikh beliefs about medical ethics
- 4.5 Lesson Player: a ready-to-go presentation with built-in resources and teacher notes
- 4 Image Gallery: a useful gallery of photos and film stills from the chapter
- 4.5 Self-Assessment Sheet: students evaluate their learning against the lesson objectives

Ideas for starters

1. Use the Starter from the *Student Book*.
2. Put the word 'cloning' on the board. Then ask students to come up with their own responses to it, plus the response that they think a Sikh would give.
3. Challenge students to come up with as many reasons as possible why cloning is controversial in three minutes.

Activity guidance

- This unit has the potential to create a number of sideline discussions – with debates about when life begins and who has the right to take or change life. These sidelines can produce some fantastic discussions and lines of argument, so if they do happen, let them run for a while and encourage rounded and developed thinking.
- Tohmev's claim that unused embryos are destroyed, whilst true in most cases, may need developing, as embryos can be saved for the future, or donated to other couples who are trying to conceive.

Ideas for plenaries

1. Use the Reflection from the *Student Book*.
2. Take a class vote on cloning, or similar, with a twist – each vote must come with a full justification about why it was chosen.
3. Ask students to discuss whether or not they think religious faith should influence ethical issues. Do they think faith provides some insight on moral conduct?
4. 'All you need is love. If you are happy, don't strive for more if it does not come naturally.' Ask students how they would respond to this statement. Then ask how a couple who are unable to conceive children naturally might respond.

Further class and homework activities

1. As homework, ask students to think about how they would respond to the issue of cloning. Would they want themselves to be cloned for future medical purposes? How would they reach their decision?
2. Ask students to use 4.5 Medical Ethics Interactive Activity on the *Sikhism OxBox Online* to demonstrate their understanding of the issues raised by this topic.
3. 4.5 Medical Ethics Film Clips A, B and C on the *Sikhism OxBox Online*.
4. 4.5 Film Worksheet on the *Sikhism OxBox Online*.
5. Further suggestions on page 76 of this book.

4.6 Friends? Relationships? Marriage?

The unit in brief

This unit looks at the different approaches within Sikhism to friendships and romantic relationships, as well as the relationship each believer has with God. It also explores the idea of a relationship and marriage as planned by God.

Key ideas

- Sikhs believe friendships and relationships are a blessing, especially if they remind them of God
- Initiated Sikhs don't 'date', but rather they believe there is someone ordained by God to be their life partner
- Guru Nanak taught on the importance of marriage, so Sikhs are encouraged to marry

Skills practised

- Thinking: thinking about the idea that members of a faith community should only marry those from that community
- Reflection: reflecting on personal attitudes towards marriage and relationships and whether it's okay to be single
- Evaluation: evaluating the responses given by individual Sikhs
- Literacy: writing a reading for a wedding

Resources:

- 4.6 Relationships Film Clip A: The Singh/Kaur family talks about the importance of having Sikh and non-Sikh friends
- 4.6 Relationships Film Clip B: The Singh/Kaur family talks about romantic relationships
- 4.6 Film Worksheet: students assess their understanding of the case study film clips by linking ideas to the *Student Book*
- 4.6 Relationships Interactive Activity: students select the sentence that most accurately describes Sikh beliefs about relationships
- 4.6 Lesson Player: a ready-to-go presentation with built-in resources and teacher notes
- 4 Image Gallery: a useful gallery of photos and film stills from the chapter
- 4.6 Self-Assessment Sheet: students evaluate their learning against the lesson objectives

Ideas for starters

1. Use the Starter from the *Student Book*.
2. Put the word 'marriage' on the board and ask for responses. Don't limit them with categories. Then ask students what they think the Sikh response might be.
3. Ask students what they value most in a friend.

Activity guidance

- Some of the activities and questions require a personal response, so it might be worthwhile monitoring how much sharing is done and how any group activities are organized.
- You could compare Sikh attitudes to relationships with those found in other faiths. For example, see Unit 5.3 in the .

Ideas for plenaries

1. Use the Reflection from the *Student Book*.
2. In pairs, ask students to imagine that they represent the Sikh faith as a whole. Explain that they have to create a statement declaring what Sikhs believe about marriage and who they should marry.
3. Ask students to come up with three key questions that, when answered, summarize what has been learned and covered in this unit.

Further class and homework activities

1. Ask students to design a reading for a wedding that contains the things they think are important for a relationship. How do these compare with the Sikh approach?
2. Ask students to use 4.6 Relationships Interactive Activity on the *Sikhism OxBox Online* to demonstrate their understanding about who Sikhs believe they should marry.
3. As homework, ask students to think about their close friends and whether or not they are a good or bad influence. Does it matter? Ask them to write a letter in support of those closest to them.
4. Show 4.6 Relationships Film Clips A and B on the *Sikhism OxBox Online* and ask for responses. Ask students whether they think marriage is based on faith as well as love.
5. 4.6 Film Worksheet on the *Sikhism OxBox Online*.
6. Further suggestions on page 76 of this book.

Chapter 4 Further Suggestions

These suggestions are addressed directly to students.

4.1 A Question of Money

1 Why do you think money has become so central to life in the UK? **

2 Create a TV advertisement to convince people that spiritual wealth and gain is much more valuable than material wealth and gain. **

3 If Guru Nanak wanted to come and retell the story of his encounter with Duni Chand tomorrow, who do you think would gain most from hearing it and why? Would you listen? ***

4 Take five key moments from the story of Duni Chand and turn them into a five-frame comic strip story or animation. *

4.2 Our Environment: Living in Harmony

1 What would happen if everyone followed the Sikh approach to the environment? Why? **

2 Create a diary entry for a frustrated teenager whose parents will not listen to his or her requests for more environmentally friendly action around their house (e.g. recycling, saving water). *

3 If you could create your own instructions about how to treat the environment, which all humans would have to follow, what would your instructions contain? *

4 Assess the value of the teachings and arguments you have looked at. Does one stand out as more valuable or useful than the others? Why? ***

4.3 Sikhism and Science: United or Divided?

1 Produce a storyboard that shows how and why science has become more and more significant in the modern world. *

2 In pairs, use mini-whiteboards and pens to have a silent discussion about how far science should be allowed to go. At least one of you should refer to a Sikh/religious argument. **

3 In your opinion, what scientific discovery would prove most useful to a religious believer (and it can't be proof that God exists!). ***

4.4 Matters of Life and Death: Abortion

1 Some people argue that there should be no medical intervention in human life at all. How would you respond to this? **

2 What does it mean to make a moral decision? *

3 Which is preferable and why – one rule that covers all of the different issues, or a range of rules which can be adapted and applied where needed? ***

4 Interview two of your classmates who you know have different views about this subject to you. Then create a Venn diagram that shows the similarities and differences between your views. ***

5 Apply what you have learned from this unit, and Unit 4.3, to the following statement: 'Abortion should be illegal in this country.' **

4.5 Medical Ethics: IVF and Cloning

1 Decide which medical ethical issue is of most concern or importance to you. Then organize a hypothetical protest or support march for it. What would your posters say? What chants would you have? **

2 Research more about the issues surrounding embryo testing. Then find out who your local MP is and write a letter to him or her, either supporting or rejecting it. ***

3 Do you believe that embryos are human life? Would you find it acceptable if your embryos were used for research? **

4 Draw on your learning about Sikh beliefs and your knowledge of at least one other faith to explain what religious people mean when they talk about the 'sanctity of life'. ***

4.6 Friends? Relationships? Marriage?

1 Write an advertisement for the position of being your friend. What would your criteria be? What would you rule out? Why? *

2 Compare the Sikh views on relationships with your own views. What are the similarities and differences? Make further comparisons with the beliefs of other faiths you have studied. ***

3 Graphically represent the views in your class about marriage, and whether or not you should be the same faith as the person you marry. *

4 Traditional perspectives would say that when you love someone, it is natural to get married to them. How would you and others respond to this? **

5 Your Sikh friend has fallen in love with a non-Sikh. Give them advice about what they should do (referring to what you have learned in this unit). **

Assessment in the *Student Book*

You will find an assessment task at the end of every chapter which focuses on AT2. In this chapter, the task asks students to write a response to a statement about the relevance of religion in the modern world.

In the *Student Book* (and on the supporting worksheets), you'll find guidance about levels of assessment that you can use to help your students understand what their work should include. You could ask them to use these criteria for self-or peer-assessment once they've completed the task.

> **Living Faiths Assessment**
>
> ***Student Book***
> - Assessment Task
> - Levels Guidance
>
> ***OxBox Online***
> - Auto-Marked Test
> - Assessment Task Presentation
> - Assessment Worksheets

Assessment Task for Chapter 4 (pages **62–63** of the *Sikhism Student Book*)

Objectives

- Explore some key questions and issues of the modern world, and identify and analyse some Sikh responses to them.
- Show understanding and awareness of significant issues in the modern world.

Task

'Religion cannot give any guidance on how to live in the modern world'. Respond to this question from the point of view of a young Sikh living in the UK today.

Write at least three paragraphs in response to the above statement. Make sure you include something about the challenges that a young Sikh would face when trying to put their faith into practice in today's world.

Assessment in *OxBox Online*

On the *Sikhism OxBox Online*, you'll find resources to use when introducing the assessment task to the class.

You can use the *Chapter 4 Assessment Task Presentation* as a front-of-class tool to help your students unpack the assessment criteria, and understand what is expected of them.

Chapter 4 Assessment Worksheets accompany the task, so that once you finish the presentation, your students can easily get started.

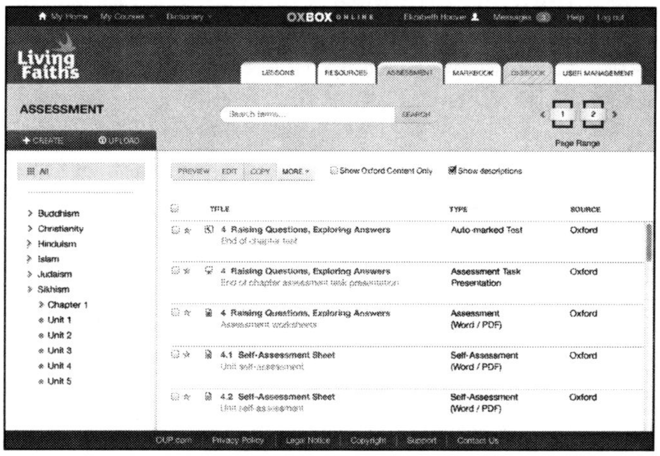

▲ Assessment resources for Chapter 4 on the *Sikhism Oxbox Online*

Auto-marked tests

The *Sikhism OxBox Online* also contains auto-marked tests for each chapter to help save you time setting questions and marking for AT1. The test for this chapter contains 15 questions and will take most students about half an hour. Test results are automatically stored in the markbook.

Digital markbook

A markbook and a reporting function complete the *OxBox Online* assessment package, so you can keep all your students' test results and assessment scores in one place. This can include the auto-marked tests as well as pieces of work you or the students have marked by hand.

Chapter 5 Overview
Sikh Beliefs in Action

Helping you deliver Key Stage 3 RE

This chapter addresses the following areas of the Programme of Study:

Key concepts

Practices and ways of life

- Exploring the impact of religions and beliefs on how people live their lives
- Understanding that religious practices are diverse, change over time and are influenced by cultures

Identity, diversity and belonging

- Understanding how individuals develop a sense of identity and belonging through faith or belief
- Exploring the variety, difference and relationships that exist within and between religions, values and beliefs

Key processes

Learning about religion

- Investigate the impact of religious beliefs and teachings on individuals, communities and societies, the reasons for commitment and the causes of diversity
- Evaluate how religious beliefs and teachings inform answers to ultimate questions and ethical issues

Learning from religion

- Reflect on the relationship between beliefs, teachings, world issues and ultimate questions
- Evaluate beliefs, commitments and the impact of religion in the contemporary world
- Express insights into the significance and value of religion and other world views for human relationships

The big picture

These are the key ideas behind this chapter:

- Following the examples of the Gurus, in particular Guru Har Gobind, Sikhism believes strongly in fighting against injustice and oppression.
- Because one of the key principles of Sikhism is to protect life, most Sikhs are against the death penalty.
- The belief that everyone is equal – regardless of gender, faith, race, or age – is fundamental to Sikh beliefs.
- Sikhs are prepared to fight, if absolutely necessary, in order to protect the innocent and vulnerable.
- Sikhism is very tolerant of other faiths and is happy to work with them for the common good of humanity.

Chapter outline

Use this to give students a mental road map of the chapter:

5.1 Fighting For Justice – uses the story of Guru Har Gobind's imprisonment as a basis for considering the issue of injustice

5.2 Massacres at Amritsar – examines the events and significance of the two Amritsar massacres in 1919 and 1984

5.3 Where Does Sikhism Stand on the Death Penalty? – introduces the issue of the death penalty and Sikh reactions to it

5.4 Is Equality the Norm? – discusses equality, particularly gender equality, and its place in Sikhism

5.5 Purely Spiritual Warriors or Actual Soldiers? – examines how Sikhism deals with the issue of conflict and its resolution

5.6 A Faith Living Amongst Faiths – considers interfaith issues and, in particular, connections between Sikhism and Hinduism and Islam

Opportunities for assessment

Summative assessments on the *Sikhism OxBox Online* include automarked tests, interactive activities, and self-assessment worksheets.

The end-of-chapter assessment task in the *Student Book* provides formative assessment. Supporting materials for the assessment task can be found on the *Sikhism OxBox Online*, such as the Assessment Task Presentation and the related worksheets.

There are other opportunities for assessment too. For example, you could use some of the activities or reflection points throughout each *Student Book* unit, or some of the 'Further Suggestions' at the end of this chapter.

Getting ready for this chapter

- This chapter and Chapter 4, in particular, require students to be able to explain and apply their own ideas and beliefs, so you could spend a lesson exploring a range of ethical issues and modern dilemmas to get them familiar with the types of questions they will be looking at, if you haven't already done so before beginning Chapter 4.
- If you have the *Sikhism OxBox Online*, watch the case study film clips in advance, so that you can prepare and guide students before and during their viewing.

Objectives and outcomes for this chapter

Objectives	Unit	Outcomes
Most students will:		Most students will be able to:
• explain the significance of the story of Guru Har Gobind • evaluate the work of UNITED SIKHS • reflect on what it takes to fight injustice.	**5.1**	• relate the story of Guru Har Gobind and explain its importance • discuss the work of UNITED SIKHS • consider their own perspective on fighting injustice.
• evaluate the importance of history to Sikhs • explain the significance of the events at Amritsar in 1984 • consider what they would do if faced with a life-or-death situation.	**5.2**	• explain the importance to Sikhs of the two massacres at Amritsar in 1919 and 1984 • evaluate the issues raised by the 1984 massacre in particular • consider their own position about fighting and possibly dying for a belief.
• identify and analyse the range of responses to the death penalty within Sikhism • explain why the death penalty is an ethical issue • consider their own views about the death penalty.	**5.3**	• explain different Sikh responses to the death penalty • explain what the death penalty is, its purposes, and its moral implications • reflect on their own views about the death penalty.
• explain Sikh beliefs about the roles of men and women • apply the teachings of key Gurus to modern Sikh families • consider where they stand on the issue of equality.	**5.4**	• discuss Sikh beliefs about gender roles • use case study examples to apply scriptural teachings to modern Sikh life • discuss their own perspective about the issue of equality.
• examine the role of Sikh soldiers, particularly in the UN • explain how Sikh beliefs influence their views on resolving conflict • reflect on their own views about ways of resolving conflicts.	**5.5**	• explain the role and aims of the UN, and the part played by Sikh soldiers • explain how Sikhs use their beliefs to approach resolving conflict • consider their own attitudes towards resolving conflict.
• examine how Sikhs understand their faith in the light of other faiths • analyse Sikh teachings about other faiths • ask questions about whether any religion can be better or more relevant than another.	**5.6**	• explain the relationship between Sikhism and other faiths, in particular Hinduism and Islam • explore Sikh teachings and suggest ways that Sikhs can apply them to other faiths • examine the place of religion in a belief in God.

5.1 Fighting For Justice

The unit in brief

The unit looks at the example of Guru Har Gobind and the Sikh principle of fighting against injustice. This is partly done by looking at the work of UNITED SIKHS.

Key ideas

- Guru Har Gobind believed in fighting against injustice
- UNITED SIKHS is a charity which fights for religious freedom
- Comparisons between the Guru's beliefs and actions and those of UNITED SIKHS.

Useful Words

altruism, injustice, justice, political prisoners

Skills practised

- Application: applying the life and example of Guru Har Gobind to the work of UNITED SIKHS
- Thinking: considering how injustice can be fought against
- Research: finding out more about Terry Waite, Nelson Mandela and Aung San Suu Kyi
- Reflection: reflecting on the moral imperative of assisting someone wrongly held in prison in another country

Resources

- 5.1 Guru Har Gobind Worksheet: students design a logo for Guru Har Gobind and the things he fought for during his life
- 5.1 Guru Har Gobind Interactive Activity: students drag events from the life of Guru Har Gobind into the correct order
- 5.1 Lesson Player: a ready-to-go presentation with built-in resources and teacher notes
- 5 Image Gallery: a useful gallery of photos and film stills from the chapter
- 5.1 Self-Assessment Sheet: students evaluate their learning against the lesson objectives

Ideas for starters

1. Use the Starter from the *Student Book*. The photos show Guru Har Gobind, Terry Waite, Nelson Mandela and Aung San Suu Kyi, all of whom were unjustly imprisoned in their lives.
2. Take the class to the library and ask them to research one or two examples of injustices from history. Then ask them how they think other people should have reacted at the time.

3. Explain to the class that altruism is 'being selflessly concerned about the welfare of others'. Ask students to give themselves a score out of ten for how altruistic they think they are. Ask for volunteers to explain their answers.

Activity guidance

- The Starter in the *Student Book* assumes that you have already done a little work on Guru Har Gobind. If this isn't the case, be ready to go through information from earlier units to get them up to speed.
- The concept of altruism is central to this unit. You may want to talk through the meaning with some of your students – encouraging them to think of someone who they would class as altruistic.

Ideas for plenaries

1. Use the Reflection from the *Student Book*.
2. Create a class continuum to display what students believe about how altruistic a person should be. Clarify all answers.
3. As a whole class, ask students to create a video message that can be played to the staff, or to the rest of the school (uploaded onto the school website), explaining the principles studied in this unit and why they could be useful for others.

Further class and homework activities

1. To assist with the Starter in the *Student Book*, you could show the photos of Guru Har Gobind, Terry Waite, Nelson Mandela and Aung San Suu Kyi in 5 Image Gallery on the *Sikhism OxBox Online*.
2. Ask students to use 5.1 Guru Har Gobind Worksheet on the *Sikhism OxBox Online* to demonstrate their understanding about the Guru. They can then compare it to the logo for UNITED SIKHS and see if there are any similarities in theme or meaning.
3. Ask students to use 5.1 Guru Har Gobind Interactive Activity on the *Sikhism OxBox Online* to consolidate their learning about Guru Har Gobind.
4. As homework, ask students to design a campaign to free Guru Har Gobind from prison. Ask what slogan(s) they would use. Tell them to think carefully about the principles he stood for and the way he put them into practice.
5. As a possible homework task, ask students to research the work of UNITED SIKHS. Which countries and issues are they most actively involved with at the moment?
6. Further suggestions on page 92 of this book.

5.2 Massacres at Amritsar

The unit in brief

This unit looks at the events of 1919 and 1984 in Amritsar, where a large number of Sikhs were killed on each occasion. It focuses on the invasion of the Golden Temple in 1984 and the aftermath of that event.

Key ideas

- There were two massacres at Amritsar, in 1919 and 1984
- In 1919 British troops opened fire on a crowd of over 10,000 Sikh pilgrims and others, killing 379 people
- In 1984 over 10,000 Sikhs were killed during Anti-Sikh riots, after the Indian Prime Minister was assassinated by two Sikh bodyguards
- Sikhs continue to ask what their response should be to the situation today

Skills practised

- Thinking: considering Sikh reactions to the events of 1984; thinking about the importance of history
- Literacy: creating an online news story
- Reflection: reflecting on the idea of dying for a belief, and also whether violence can ever bring peace

Resources

- 5.2 Amritsar Worksheet: students create a front page for a newspaper that covers these events
- 5.2 Amritsar Interactive Activity: students order opinions about the massacres at Amritsar according to how far they agree with them
- 5.2 Lesson Player: a ready-to-go presentation with built-in resources and teacher notes
- 5 Image Gallery: a useful gallery of photos and film stills from the chapter
- 5.2 Self-Assessment Sheet: students evaluate their learning against the lesson objectives

Ideas for starters

1. Use the Starter from the *Student Book*.
2. Put a range of categories on the board, such as family, friends, a million pounds, football team, pop band of the moment (whoever it is!). Then ask students to suggest what they would be prepared to give up in order to obtain, retain, or keep safe the things on the board.
3. Ask students to think back to the British riots of summer 2011. Did they think they were a good thing or a bad thing? Aim to find out their attitudes towards protesting and what it can achieve.

Activity guidance

- This unit deals with sensitive, and sometimes controversial, topics within Sikhism and needs to be handled with care. You may want to do a little further reading on this before you start teaching.
- A quick geography lesson could be useful here to show students where the region of Punjab is, and to give context to the story.
- The Reflection is a whole-class activity. You may find it useful to complete the snowball process with students first (individual to pairs to fours and so on), so that they are all more comfortable with expressing their ideas.

Ideas for plenaries

1. Use the Reflection from the *Student Book*.
2. Ask students to look back over the learning they have completed for this unit and write a short summary at the end to explain how well they think they have achieved the unit's Learning Objectives.
3. Ask students, in pairs, to look back over the events covered by this unit and ask themselves the question: 'Could something similar happen again?' If so, where and why and if not, why not?
4. Ask students to revisit the starter in light of their learning in the lesson and consider how far people really do learn lessons from past events.

Further class and homework activities

1. As homework, ask students to research what happened at Amritsar in 1984 in more detail. They should try to find at least three different sources, and use them to create a diary entry, as if they are Sikhs, explaining why this had such an impact on them and their faith.
2. Ask students to do some research to find out about conscientious objectors and their reasons for not fighting in World War Two. Remember that pacifists are not necessarily motivated by religious beliefs.
3. Ask students to use 5.2 Amritsar Worksheet on the *Sikhism OxBox Online* to further illustrate their awareness of the events of 1984 as they happened. Encourage further research and reading if this hasn't already been done.
4. Ask students to use 5.2 Amritsar Interactive Activity on the *Sikhism OxBox Online* to consolidate their learning about the events of 1984.
5. Further suggestions on page 92 of this book.

5.3 Where Does Sikhism Stand on the Death Penalty?

The unit in brief

This unit looks at Sikh responses to the controversial topic of the death penalty. It also explores a recent case involving the sentencing of a Sikh to death in India.

Key ideas

- The death penalty is the legalized killing of a criminal by the government of a country
- Most Sikhs are against the death penalty
- There was a recent case of a Sikh sentenced to death in India

Useful Words

death row, deterrent, inhumane, Nishan Sahib, persecution

Skills practised

- Thinking: contemplating the issues and beliefs surrounding the death penalty; considering the aims of punishment; considering the role of religions in political issues
- Reflection: reflecting on students' own attitudes towards the death penalty
- Evaluation: evaluating the arguments given by Sikhs in response to this issue

Resources

- 5.3 Death Penalty Worksheet: students create a set of cards for a debate, share them and then order the cards they receive in return
- 5.3 Death Penalty Interactive Activity: students select true statements describing Sikh beliefs about the death penalty
- 5.3 Lesson Player: a ready-to-go presentation with built-in resources and teacher notes
- 5 Image Gallery: a useful gallery of photos and film stills from the chapter
- 5.3 Self-Assessment Sheet: students evaluate their learning against the lesson objectives

Ideas for starters

1. Use the Starter from the *Student Book*.
2. Show students an image of an electric chair, or the lethal injection machinery, and ask them for their responses.
3. Ask students to turn to a partner and discuss whether or not they think the death penalty should be reinstated in the UK. This can be followed up at the end of the lesson.

Activity guidance

- This is quite an emotive topic, and can produce some controversial viewpoints about certain groups in society. Be ready for this and any other unexpected contributions; have strategies in place to deal with them. It's a very worthwhile discussion, and Sikh responses to issues of life and death match many others.
- You could compare Sikh attitudes to the death penalty with those in Islam. See Unit 4.7 in the *Islam Student Book*.

Ideas for plenaries

1. Use the Reflection from the *Student Book*.
2. At the end of the lesson, follow up Starter 3 above, by holding a class debate and vote (as if students are MPs) about whether the death penalty should be reinstated in the UK.
3. Ask students to consider whether or not they have met the Learning Objectives for this unit. If so, how and if not, what do they need to do.
4. Ask students to consider the idea that restitution (putting things right) is better than punishing someone. Ask them to suggest how this approach could be introduced into a school, giving examples of how it could work.

Further class and homework activities

1. Ask students to use 5.3 Death Penalty Worksheet on the *Sikhism OxBox Online* to produce and answer a key question about the death penalty.
2. Ask students to use 5.3 Death Penalty Interactive Activity on the *Sikhism OxBox Online* to demonstrate their understanding of Sikh responses to the death penalty.
5. Further suggestions on page 92 of this book.

5.4 Is Equality the Norm?

The unit in brief

This unit uses a case study to examine the teachings, beliefs and practices that Sikhs refer to when considering issues of equality.

Key ideas

- Sikh teachings about equality hold that everyone is equal, regardless of gender, faith, race or age
- Sikh women have equal rights and freedoms as men

Skills practised

- Literacy: analysing a quotation from scripture
- Thinking: considering Sikh beliefs about equality and whether they reflect the student's own ideas
- Reflection: reflecting on the student's own attitudes towards equality

Resources

- 5.4 Equality Audio Clip: a recording about equality from the Guru Granth Sahib, page 473
- 5.4 Equality Worksheet: students create a radio script in order to explore the different attitudes towards equality, especially between men and women
- 5.4 Equality Interactive Activity: students fill the gaps in a paragraph about equality
- 5.4 Lesson Player: a ready-to-go presentation with built-in resources and teacher notes
- 5 Image Gallery: a useful gallery of photos and film stills from the chapter
- 5.4 Self-assessment Sheet: students evaluate their learning against the lesson objectives

Ideas for starters

1. Use the Starter from the *Student Book*.
2. Put the word 'equality' on the board and ask students to think about it and respond. Don't limit their responses – see what comes out.
3. Ask students to comment on any issues of equality that they feel they have been part of. This will need careful management.

Activity guidance

- This could be a sensitive topic for many, and could yield some difficult responses from some students. However, it's also a topic that could produce some very effective and useful RE in a social and emotional context.
- You may wish to compare Sikh attitudes to men and women with those in Islam. See Unit 5.2 in the *Islam Student Book*.

Ideas for plenaries

1. Use the Reflection from the *Student Book*.
2. Ask students to silently write down their own responses to the unit. Don't give them boundaries or direction; just ask for a response. You may only get one word, or you may get an essay!
3. Ask students if they feel as though they have met the unit's Learning Objectives. If so, how and if not, what could they do to change that?
4. Ask students to consider the following: is there a difference between treating people the same way and giving people an equal opportunity in life? Are there examples when it is right to treat people differently to ensure they have an equal opportunity?

Further class and homework activities

1. Ask students to do some research into the recent debate in the Anglican Church about women bishops looking at the arguments that are given both for and against. They should then create a role-play script for a conversation between a Sikh and an Anglican who believes that it is not acceptable for women to become bishops.
2. 5.4 Equality Audio Clip on the *Sikhism OxBox Online*.
3. Ask students to use 5.4 Equality Worksheet *Sikhism OxBox Online* to create a radio script exploring different attitudes towards equality.
4. Ask students to use 5.4 Equality Interactive Activity on the *Sikhism OxBox Online* to demonstrate their understanding of Sikh attitudes towards equality.
5. Further suggestions on page 92 of this book.

5.5 Purely Spiritual Warriors or Actual Soldiers?

The unit in brief

This unit uses case study quotations to look at different ways in which Sikhs respond to conflict. It also includes an exploration of the role of Sikh soldiers in the UN and the British Army.

Key ideas

- Sikhs respond to conflict in different ways
- The Singh family offered practical aid during the riots of August 2011
- There are Sikhs in the armed forces and peacekeeping troops

Skills practised

- Thinking: contemplating the issues and beliefs surrounding the involvement of Sikhs in conflict or the military
- Literacy: writing a newspaper report about the 2011 riots
- Application: applying previous knowledge to the issue of conflict
- Research: finding out more about the UN and the Declaration of Human Rights
- Reflection: reflecting on the student's own attitudes towards conflict

Resources

- 5.5 Conflict Film Clip: Balwir Singh and his father talk about how Sikhs got involved to defend their communities during the 2011 summer riots
- 5.5 Film Worksheet: students assess their understanding of the case study film clip by linking ideas to the *Student Book*
- 5.5 Conflict Interactive Activity: students link Sikh beliefs about conflict with how they influence people
- 5.5 Lesson Player: a ready-to-go presentation with built-in resources and teacher notes
- 5 Image Gallery: a useful gallery of photos and film stills from the chapter
- 5.5 Self-Assessment Sheet: students evaluate their learning against the lesson objectives

Ideas for starters

1. Use the Starter from the *Student Book*.
2. Show the class still images or short film clips from the 2011 summer riots. Then ask students to respond from both a personal viewpoint and from that of a Sikh.
3. Ask students discuss whether or not people of faith should be part of the armed forces. What justifications could there be for this?

Activity guidance

- It is important to emphasize that the views expressed in the *Student Book* unit do not cover all of the different approaches that a Sikh might have towards conflict, and that there will always be variety. Encourage students to consider all they have learned about Sikh beliefs so far in their studies, and to apply those principles to this issue to see what different outcomes and judgments they can put forward.
- You may wish to compare Sikh attitudes to conflict with those of Christianity, in particular pacifism. See Unit 4.5 in the *Christianity Student Book*.

Ideas for plenaries

1. Use the Reflection from the *Student Book*.
2. Tell all students to stand up and then ask them a series of 'yes' and 'no' questions about this topic – they remain standing for 'yes', and sit down for 'no'. The questions could be factual or opinion-based.
3. Ask students to consider whether or not they have met the unit's Learning Objectives. If so, how, and if not, what do they need to do.

Further class and homework activities

1. Ask students to use 5.5 Conflict Interactive Activity on the *Sikhism OxBox Online* to demonstrate their understanding of Sikh responses to conflict.
2. 5.5 Conflict Film Clip on the *Sikhism OxBox Online*.
3. 5.5 Film Worksheet on the *Sikhism OxBox Online*.
4. Further suggestions on page 92 of this book.

5.6 A Faith Living Amongst Faiths

The unit in brief

This unit explores different teachings and examples from the Gurus to examine how Sikhism understands and interacts with other faiths.

Key ideas

- Guru Nanak was against religious conflict
- Guru Nanak affirmed that all those that believe in One God, irrespective of their religion, are the creation of God
- Sikhs believe that no humans are superior to others
- Some Sikhs are actively involved in interfaith work

Skills practised

- Comparison: examining similarities and differences between the beliefs of other faiths
- Literacy: analysing quotations from scripture
- Reflection: reflecting on whether religion itself is necessary, or just God

Resources

- 5.6 Other Faiths Audio Clip: a recording from the Guru Granth Sahib, pages 611–612
- 5.6 Other Faiths Worksheet: students create a statement as if from a Sikh organization, explaining their response to interfaith work
- 5.6 Other Faiths Interactive Activity: students select statements that most accurately describe what Sikhism teaches about other faiths
- 5.6 Lesson Player: a ready-to-go presentation with built-in resources and teacher notes
- 5 Image Gallery: a useful gallery of photos and film stills from the chapter
- 5.6 Self-Assessment Sheet: students evaluate their learning against the lesson objectives

Ideas for starters

1. Use the Starter from the *Student Book*.
2. Get students to put a range of film, TV or music characters on the board and start drawing lines between them all to show who would work with whom and why. Encourage them to start thinking about how the more unusual or unexpected ones would connect up successfully.
3. Test students' knowledge and understanding. Without letting them look through any books, ask them to suggest answers to the question: 'How does Sikhism view other faiths?'

Activity guidance

- The starter activities in the *Student Book* are designed to make students think. It might be an idea to hand out mini-whiteboards or large pieces of paper and ask students to write down ideas in response to the questions. They could then compare and contrast their ideas with others before formulating a final response.
- The Reflection in the *Student Book* is a group activity and involves students sharing their personal reflections. You may want to organize the groups yourself.

Ideas for plenaries

1. Use the Reflection from the *Student Book*.
2. Ask students to produce a role-play that includes a conversation between two Sikhs about their interfaith work and the reasons for it.
3. Ask students to design a flier, based on the teachings they have learned from this unit, that could be posted out or emailed to all local faith centres to encourage interfaith work.

Further class and homework activities

1. Ask students to research the activities of a local Faith Forum or similar organization. They should answer the following questions: What are their aims? What have they achieved? Who is involved?
2. Ask students to identify some ways Youth Forums and schools could be involved in work to help different faiths and other groups in the community to work together. What sort of things would such groups get involved with?
3. 5.6 Other Faiths Audio Clip on the *Sikhism OxBox Online*.
4. Ask students to use 5.6 Other Faiths Worksheet on the *Sikhism OxBox Online* to further illustrate their understanding about how many Sikhs approach interfaith issues.
5. Ask students to use 5.6 Other Faiths Interactive Activity on the *Sikhism OxBox Online* to consolidate their learning about the role of other faiths in the work of Sikhism.
6. Further suggestions on page 92 of this book.

Chapter 5 Further Suggestions

These suggestions are addressed directly to students.

5.1 Fighting For Justice

1 Research the current projects that Amnesty International is involved in. Choose the one that you think is the most worthy and explain why. *

2 Why do you think power causes people to behave in such terrible ways? **

3 Create a mock TV advert to convince people that they should try to make a difference to their global community. **

5.2 Massacres at Amritsar

1 Find out what the latest difficulties have been between religion and government in a country of your choice. Explain the facts around them and reflect on your findings. **

2 Create a diary entry for a Sikh who was present at Amritsar during the events of 1984. Try to explore the different emotions that they would have been feeling. **

3 If you could create an environment where no conflict existed between groups, what would it be like and how would you get it to that point? ***

4 Choose five key moments from the events at Amritsar in 1983-4 and write key questions and observations about each one. For example, why did this happen at this particular moment? What could have been done to prevent this? Swap questions with a partner and use them to discuss the events. **

5.3 Where Does Sikhism Stand on the Death Penalty?

1 In pairs, use mini-whiteboards and pens to have a silent discussion about the death penalty. **

2 Assess the value of the teachings and arguments you have looked at. Does one stand out as more valuable or useful than the others? **

5.4 Is Equality the Norm?

1 Some people argue that men and women should have totally different roles. How would you respond to this? **

2 What do you think equality means? *

3 Connect together all of the arguments that you have identified for this topic. Which one would you say is the strongest, and which one is the weakest? Why? **

4 Interview two of your classmates with different views about equality to you. Then create a Venn diagram that shows the similarities and differences between your views. ***

5.5 Purely Spiritual Warriors or Actual Soldiers?

1 Write an advertisement for the position of a Sikh soldier. What would your criteria be? What would you rule out? Why? **

2 What is the difference between a spiritual warrior and an actual soldier? Which do you think is the hardest role? ***

3 Graphically represent the views in your class about conflict, and whether or not a religious believer should fight in a war. **

4 Have a debate with a partner about the claim that conflict can be resolved through fighting. **

5.6 A Faith Living Amongst Faiths

1 Suggest ways in which all of the main faiths could work together. What might they try to achieve? **

2 Write a letter from a Sikh community to other religious communities, which highlights the shared beliefs that exist between them. ***

3 Design a symbol that reflects all six main world religions. ***

4 Write the timetable for a meeting of all the faith groups in your area. Consider the practical arrangements for such a meeting. Where will they meet? Who will lead the meeting? What food and drink will be served? What will the aims be? ***

Chapter 5 Assessment

Assessment in the *Student Book*

You will find an assessment task at the end of every chapter which focuses on AT2. In this chapter, the task asks students to write a news article for a smartphone news app from the point of view of a Sikh.

In the *Student Book* (and on the supporting worksheets), you'll find guidance about levels of assessment that you can use to help your students understand what their work should include. You could ask them to use these criteria for self or peer assessment once they've completed the task.

Living Faiths Assessment

Student Book

- Assessment Task
- Levels Guidance

OxBox Online

- Auto-Marked Test
- Assessment Task Presentation
- Assessment Worksheets

Assessment Task for Chapter 5 (pages **76–77** of the *Sikhism Student Book*)

Objectives

- Explain how religious teachings guide Sikhs' moral and ethical actions and choices.
- Reflect on and identify where guidance and direction can come from in life.

Task

'My faith: It is all I need.'

Your task is to write a news article for a smartphone news app from the point of view of a Sikh, using the statement above as the headline.

Assessment in *OxBox Online*

On the *Sikhism OxBox Online*, you'll find resources to use when introducing the assessment task to the class.

You can use the *Chapter 5 Assessment Task Presentation* as a front-of-class tool to help your students unpack the assessment criteria, and understand what is expected of them.

Chapter 5 Assessment Worksheets accompany the task, so that once you finish the presentation, your students can easily get started.

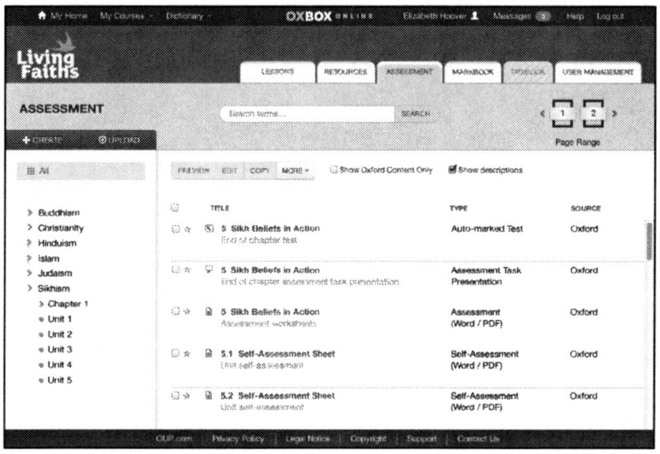

▲ Assessment resources for Chapter 5 on the *Sikhism Oxbox Online*

Auto-marked tests

The *Sikhism OxBox Online* also contains auto-marked tests for each chapter to help save you time setting questions and marking for AT1. The test for this chapter contains 15 questions and will take most students about half an hour. Test results are automatically stored in the markbook.

Digital markbook

A markbook and a reporting function complete the OxBox Online assessment package, so you can keep all your students' test results and assessment scores in one place. This can include the auto-marked tests as well as pieces of work you or the students have marked by hand.

Glossary

Abortion Medically removing a baby from the womb during pregnancy
Akal Purakh A Sikh name for God
Altruism Selfless care and concern for others
Amrit Sanskar The initiation ceremony
Anand Sanskar The marriage ceremony
Antam Sanskar The funeral ceremony
Biodiversity The variety of life in a particular place
Castes Groups and/or divisions within society with higher or lower status than each other
Chaur An implement like a fly whisk that is used to pay respect to the Guru Granth Sahib
Cloning Cultivating DNA to make an exact copy of a living creature
Conception The moment that a sperm fertilizes an egg and a woman becomes pregnant
Creeds Statements of belief, usually religious
Daswandh Giving a tenth of one's salary as a charitable donation
Death row The part of a prison housing those sentenced to death
Deterrent To deter or put others off from committing a crime
Dhan Giving to charity or giving time to others
Embryo testing Scientific testing on a foetus at very early stages of development, usually for medical research
Euthanasia Helping someone else to die
Granthi Someone who is fluent in reading the Guru Granth Sahib
Gurbani Teachings of the Guru found in the Guru Granth Sahib and other religious texts
Gurdwara The Sikh place of worship
Gurmukh Putting God at the centre of your life
Guru A spiritual teacher
Guru Granth Sahib The eternal Guru of the Sikhs, which embodies the teachings of the ten Sikh Gurus
Guru Nanak The founder of Sikhism
Harmony Agreement in thought and deed
Inhumane Cruel; lacking compassion
Injustice Violation of the rights of others
IVF In-vitro fertilization; this treatment helps couples to have children by fertilizing the egg outside the womb and then implanting it back into the woman
Janam Naam Sanskar The naming ceremony
Jakara Sikh salutation
Justice Moral righteousness
Kachera One of the Five Ks; a type of Sikh under-shorts
Kangha One of the Five Ks; a wooden comb
Kara One of the Five Ks; an iron bracelet
Karma A combination of a person's actions, with either a positive or negative outcome in the next life
Kesh One of the Five Ks; uncut hair
Khanda An important Sikh symbol containing three swords and a circle with different meanings
Kirpan One of the Five Ks; a sword
Langar Both the food and the hall in which it is served, at a gurdwara
Man Mental service, such as studying
Manmukh Putting human and materialistic desires at the centre of your life
Meditation Extended thought and contemplation
Mela A big fair or gathering
Mool Mantar The opening prayer in the Guru Granth Sahib, containing the essence of Sikhism, and describing the attributes of God
Mukti Union of the soul with God
Nagar Kirtan A parade led by five Sikhs, to represent the Panj Piare (see Unit 2.6)
Nishan Sahib The Sikh flag
Palki The canopy covering the Guru Granth Sahib
Persecution Persistent ill-treatment, usually because of race or religion

Pilgrimage A holy journey to a place of religious significance
Political prisoners People imprisoned for their political beliefs or actions
Reht Maryada The Sikh code of conduct
Reincarnation A cycle of birth and death and rebirth
Religious experience An experience of God; a spiritual experience
Sacred Holy, or a gift from God
Sacred thread A cord worn as a Hindu rite of passage
Sangat A Sikh congregation
Secular Without religious reference; non-religious
Seva (sewa) Selfless service to God's creation
Shabad The Word of God in Gurbani
Simran Meditating on the word of God; for Sikhs, this must also be completed to balance out seva – to remember God in everything
Soul (atma) The spiritual spark that keeps the body alive
Sustainable Able to be maintained
Takht The 'throne' on which the Guru Granth Sahib is placed
Tan Physical service, for example in the langar

OXFORD
UNIVERSITY PRESS

Great Clarendon Street, Oxford OX2 6DP

Oxford University Press is a department of the University of Oxford.
It furthers the University's objective of excellence in research,
scholarship, and education by publishing worldwide in

Oxford New York

Auckland Cape Town Dar es Salaam Hong Kong Karachi
Kuala Lumpur Madrid Melbourne Mexico City Nairobi
New Delhi Shanghai Taipei Toronto

With offices in

Argentina Austria Brazil Chile Czech Republic France Greece
Guatemala Hungary Italy Japan Poland Portugal Singapore
South Korea Switzerland Thailand Turkey Ukraine Vietnam

Oxford is a registered trade mark of Oxford University Press
in the UK and in certain other countries

First published 2013

British Library Cataloguing in Publication Data

Data available

ISBN-13: 978-0-19-838902 6

10 9 8 7 6 5 4 3 2 1

Printed by Bell & Bain Ltd, Glasgow

Acknowledgements

The publishers would like to thank the following for permission to use their photographs:

Cover: Narinder Singh

From the author, Julie Haigh: Many thanks to both the families who have helped shape this book with their openness and faith. It has been a pleasure to work with you. Thanks also to Janice Chan, Lois Durrant, Minh Ha Duong and Janet Dyson for their help and support. The greatest thanks go to my wonderful family, Dom and Maia, who have been an endless source of inspiration, encouragement and love. And, of course, even more cups of tea.

OUP wishes to thank the Singh/Kaur family, the Singh family and Mejindarpal Kaur for agreeing to take part in the case study films and to be photographed for this title. We would also like to thank Mejindarpal Kaur and her dedicated team at UNITED SIKHS for reviewing this book.

FSC www.fsc.org MIX Paper from responsible sources FSC® C007785